D1351497

WARDROBE WISDOM

From a Royal Lady's Maid

WARDROBE WISDOM

From a Royal Lady's Maid

*How to dress and take
care of your clothes*

ALICIA HEALEY

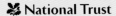

National Trust

For N.J.H.

First published in the United Kingdom in 2018 by
National Trust Books
43 Great Ormond Street
London WC1N 3HZ

An imprint of Pavilion Books Company Ltd

Text © Alicia Healey, 2018
Volume © National Trust Books, 2018

Illustrations by Willa Gebbie

ISBN: 9781911358435

A CIP catalogue record for this book is available from the British Library.

10 9 8 7 6 5 4 3 2 1

Reproduction by Rival Colour Ltd, UK
Printed by 1010 Printing International Ltd, China

This book can be ordered direct from the publisher at the website
www.pavilionbooks.com, or try your local bookshop.

Also available at National Trust shops or
www.shop.nationaltrust.org.uk

Contents

Part III – Care of Clothing and Accessories

Introduction

Vain trifles as they seem, clothes have, they say, more important offices than to merely keep us warm. They change our view of the world and the world's view of us.

ORLANDO, VIRGINIA WOOLF

Ladies of wealth in possession of extensive wardrobes are the kinds of ladies who might require the services of a modern-day lady's maid. How else to manage the rows of handbags with five-figure price tags, shelves of shoes from floor to ceiling, endless rails of exquisite couture dresses and bespoke tailoring all hanging in line waiting for their next outing? Wardrobes of this scale are like museums – their valuable contents should be cared for, worn, seen and loved. Curating clothing is a lady's maid's work. That was one of the skills I learned within the Royal Household at Buckingham Palace over the four years I worked there. After I left, I became a style connoisseur and expert in all manner of clothing crises and wardrobe woes. I have criss-crossed the globe with Saudi Arabian clients, both rich and royal, where my duties included organising vast wardrobes, caring for clothes and accessories, packing suitcases and styling the perfect outfit. My travels have broadened my wardrobe as well as my mind – from acquiring the obligatory black *abaya* dress for a trip to Riyadh, to finding the right ballgown for guests reeling with the royals at Balmoral Castle – there are very few clothing crises that I haven't faced!

I became captivated by the glamour of clothes as a child. Given a dressing-up box of my mum's old clothing, I would squabble with my sister over trying on shoes and elegant dresses that swamped my child's frame and spend hours tidying my grandma's silk scarf drawer and jewellery box. I watched costume dramas and period films just to revel in the elegance of their clothes, in sharp contrast to the utilitarian casual style of the 1990s. Turning away from the sportswear, clunky shoes and lack of colour that dominated the shops as I grew up, I looked to women with timeless style – Jackie Kennedy, Eva Peron, Grace Kelly, Princess Diana.

Clothes are an avenue for being creative with our personal style and so reflect our individual personalities and moods. I have always been aware of the transformative power of clothing to change how we feel – whether it be a professional look to give confidence at work, or dressing up for a special event. Even casual clothes – the trusty favourites you return to over and over again – are like a comfort blanket and when I'm properly dressed, I feel my best self.

I developed a more mindful approach to shopping and looking after my own clothes after becoming startled by the millions of garments that end up in landfill sites each year. I kicked the hoarding habit and now have a classic capsule wardrobe that's easily transportable across seasons, countries and cultures. In 2014 I started my blog 'The Lady's Maid', and in 2017 an Instagram account to share my tips on style and clothing care. Now I have queries every day from Bahrain to Baltimore asking for advice on what to wear to different events, what to pack for trips, how to get rid of a stubborn stain and how to save that favourite cardigan from the ubiquitous enemy of all knitwear: the pesky moth.

In this book, I will provide practical guidance on how to create the perfect wardrobe space for your clothing needs, how to effectively organise your clothing within your wardrobe, how to care for you clothing and accessories, and how to dress for any occasion. Clothing is part of our everyday lives – everyone has to make choices on what clothes to buy and wear. Whether you're a fashionista with a shoe collection to compete with Imelda Marcos, or have no interest in fashion until beset with what-on-earth-to-wear anxiety, my approach transforms even the most modest of wardrobes so that you can start to cherish the garments you own and dress effortlessly. If you would like to step into the (perfectly polished) shoes of Downton's Lady Mary and have your very own Anna to help with all your wardrobe woes, then read on for Wardrobe Wisdom from The Lady's Maid.

THE LADY'S MAID

PART I
HOW TO DRESS

Dress codes

You can never be overdressed or overeducated.

OSCAR WILDE

I would venture to say that most women have thought to themselves, 'I have nothing to wear', when faced with an invitation to an event. And should this event come with a dress code, this dressing anxiety goes up a notch. Dress codes usually appear on invitations to formal events in order to guide the recipient on what to wear, so that you don't arrive under or overdressed. While Oscar Wilde might have been right in the matter of education, I am of the opinion that it is indeed possible to be overdressed.

White tie

For example, if attending a reception in the presence
of the Queen and the dress code stated 'Lounge Suit',
it would be bad etiquette to arrive in a state of dress
more formal than this. The wording of the dress code
on invitations relates to the men's dress, e.g. 'White Tie',
'Black Tie', 'Morning Suit', 'Lounge Suit'. These all, in their
literal interpretation, refer to what the man should wear,
so it is understandable that some twenty-first-century
ladies might be somewhat uncertain as to what the
female equivalent should be. Men's fashion is always more
uniform in nature: a black tie suit is a black tie suit, and
the same one can be pulled out of the wardrobe event after
event. The trouble (and fun) for the lady is that female
fashion changes at a faster pace and there is an almost
infinite variety of dresses, in terms of colour, style and
detail, that are available for women when interpreting the
same dress code. Add to that the pressure and expectation
to wear a new dress to each event and the result is the
modern-day what-to-wear dilemma.

Formal dress

White tie
White tie is the most formal of dress codes. It is rarely
seen today and is reserved mainly for royal occasions,
such as state banquets and other royal ceremonies and
state occasions.
• Ladies should wear a full-length, formal evening dress,
with matching elegant shoes and bag.
• Tiaras can be worn – though traditionally only worn by
married women.
• Long gloves were traditionally worn with sleeveless
dresses, but they're not compulsory now.
• If a coat is needed it should be a smart evening coat –

capes, wraps or faux fur shrugs work best with white tie.
• Shoes should be either heeled courts or sandals. When
wearing closed-toe shoes, satin, velvet or metallic leather
are the best options – plain leather or suede can look
too casual.
• Jewellery – white tie is traditionally accessorised with
extravagant jewels. The glitzier the better. If you have
fancy family jewels, now is the time to wear them.

Black tie
This dress code is similar to white tie for ladies but less
formal and is still frequently seen today at formal dinners,
receptions and balls.
• Ladies should wear an evening dress or a matching
evening top and long skirt.

Black tie

- Shorter dresses are acceptable but should be of a decent knee or midi length and dressy enough to distinguish from a cocktail dress, i.e. if you are going short, then go glitzy.
- Tiaras are not worn.
- Shoes – closed-toe heels or sandals, as with white tie.

Cocktail dress
- Short dress – mini to knee-length is acceptable.

If in doubt, a little black dress is a great wardrobe staple to have as a cocktail dress – it can be easily dressed up and down, depending on the event.

- Accessories – costume jewellery is great for dressing up plain cocktail dresses – go for either statement earrings or a statement necklace.

Cocktail dress

Morning dress

Morning dress

Morning dress is the most formal day dress code (also
known as 'formal day dress'). It is still frequently used
on invitations for day events, e.g. weddings, Royal Ascot,
royal garden parties, investitures.

• Ladies should wear either a formal day dress with
matching jacket/coat or a smart two-piece suit.

• Dresses can be worn without a jacket, but they should
have a reasonable sleeve length.

• Check dress codes for the specific event – some may
require hats/headpieces (e.g. the Royal Enclosure at Royal
Ascot), but for other events it may not be necessary to
wear a hat.

• Morning dress is a day dress code, so avoid too much
evening-style fabric in the dress and accessories, e.g. satin
or velvet.

• Closed-toe court heels in suede or leather are the
most appropriate footwear, but peep-toe is acceptable in

summer. Avoid strappy sandals.

• Bags can be a clutch or a small handbag.
• Jewellery – diamonds can be a bit dressy for the daytime. Semi-precious stones and pearls are the most appropriate choice.

Top tips for formal daywear dressing

• Stick to two colours – one for the outfit and one for accessories.
• Neutral accessories are great for formal dressing – nude, ivory and black will go with outfits of most colours.
• Avoid bright colours unless you accessorise neutrally.
• The royals are wise to be seen mainly in all shades of neutral – it may seem boring, but it is hard not to look elegant in oyster or champagne.
• Avoid flimsy fascinators, such as a feather stuck on an

Formal daywear

Alice band – they add nothing to the style of an outfit.
If you don't want to wear a hat, choose a headpiece with
a substantial base.

• If you have chosen a flamboyant statement hat, let the
hat speak for itself and stick to a simple, unfussy dress and
accessories.

• Traditionally, sleeves of dresses for formal daywear
should be of a reasonable length, so if your dress is
sleeveless, a neutral cropped jacket works well with
most colours.

• Avoid cardigans for formal events (unless they are
cropped and slim-fitting, and you are young enough to
carry them off), as they're a bit too casual as a cover-up
over a formal dress.

Informal dress

Lounge suit

As a dress code, 'Lounge Suit' can be seen on either a
day or an evening invitation. It is much more casual
than morning dress and can be interpreted quite widely
for ladies.

• If the event is in the evening, a smart short evening/
cocktail dress would be appropriate.

• For daytime events, a day dress or a smart blouse and
skirt, or jacket and skirt, is suitable, or a trouser suit.

• Choose colours/prints appropriate to the occasion –
i.e. if it is a business event, your choice of colour would
perhaps be more sober than for a more social event.

• Wrap dresses and shirt dresses are good options, as they
are slightly more casual than other dresses, so are a good
choice for bridging dress codes.

• If it is an after-work event, office wear can be smartened
up with higher heels and smaller handbags, and jewellery.

Lounge suit

Smart casual

Smart casual can be hard to define because it is something of an oxymoron, so can be the trickiest dress code to interpret. The overall look should be informal, but you should still appear neat and styled, as if you've dressed for an event rather than a visit to the supermarket. Dress according to the weather, the event and the time of day. Casual doesn't mean sweatpants and trainers. Jeans might be appropriate for some events, as long as they are smart, have no rips and are worn with the right top and shoes. If it is a summer event, something like a floral dress with jacket or cardigan, wedges and small handbag would be suitable. A handled bag is preferable to a clutch – clutches tend to smarten up the look too much, so are best reserved for the smarter dress codes. Accessories can be used to 'dress up' or 'dress down' an outfit – you may have a dress that is suitable for a 'lounge suit' event when worn with smart heels and handbag, and then wear the dress again with a lower heel and a larger bag for a more casual look. Pay attention to accessories with this dress code: they can smarten up even the most casual of outfits.

Smart casual

The Season in the twenty-first century

Once sure of being among those strolling on this select and sacred lawn, every woman attending concentrated on finery that would make her the cynosure of male eyes – and the envy of all women.

ANNE DE COURCY ON ROYAL ASCOT LADIES IN 1939: *THE LAST SEASON*

In a fashion age where anything goes, I am relieved that there are still some occasions where one has to follow certain rules before getting dressed. Many of these occasions can be found within the British Season. The 'Season' refers to the calendar of sporting and cultural events that take place in England during the spring and summer months each year. The Chelsea Flower Show at the end of May is generally considered to mark the beginning of the Season. These events were traditionally attended by debutantes, and whether the event was sporting or cultural by nature, the main attraction for these debs was neither: the primary aim was for the debutantes to find a husband. This blatant husband-hunting may have died out with the debs, but the events of the British Season remain fixed and are still loyally attended. Dress codes may have relaxed for some events but most do still require attendees to 'dress up'. *Her Ladyship's Guide to the British Season* by Caroline Taggart (National Trust, 2013) comprehensively explores the full list of events that make up the British Season, so I will focus here on a few events that are quintessentially British or royal, and the ones most likely to present what-to-wear anxiety.

RHS Chelsea Flower Show

The summer Season kicks off with the Royal Horticultural Society's Chelsea Flower Show towards the end of May, showcasing the finest in horticultural design. There is no formal dress code, but a flower show is a perfect time to bring colour to one's wardrobe – think floral prints and petal pinks – so leave the stuffy suit in the office and pay tribute to the range of colour that spring blooms bring. But exercise an elegant restraint – the real flowers are the stars of the show, so if you want to wear a floral design, choose a discreet print – you don't want to look like a flowerbed yourself. If the weather permits, a floral day dress or plain top and floral skirt would be an appropriate choice for ladies. Long-sleeved wrap dresses and shirt

Chelsea Flower Show

dresses are good choices as they tend to be in lightweight fabrics so are perfect for spring. Flat shoes or a small heel are advisable. The Season may be predictable in the timing of its annual events, but sadly British seasons are less so – spring should be in the air by May, but if April showers have crept in, a lightweight mac or trench coat is advisable to have to hand.

Royal Ascot

Royal Ascot still adheres to strict dress codes for race-goers, at least within the Royal Enclosure. However, it is now the case that even at this most sartorial of race meetings, many people wear clothes that are more suitable for an evening out than for daywear; there is a time and a place for bodycon satin and open-toe stilettos, and it isn't amongst horses.

The dress code for the Royal Enclosure at Royal Ascot is basically 'formal daywear', which is defined as:

- Skirt/dress to be knee-length or longer.
- Straps on dresses should be at least one inch.
- Trouser suits are allowed, but they should be of matching colour and material.
- Hats should be worn – head pieces are acceptable as long as the base is 4in (10cm) in diameter.

What not to wear:
- Dresses of the strapless, spaghetti strap, halterneck or off-the-shoulder variety.
- Fascinators.

Other enclosures are more relaxed, e.g. strappy dresses and fascinators are permitted within the Queen Anne

Royal Ascot

Enclosure and Village Enclosure. Ascot is all about the hats, especially on Ladies' Day – the Thursday of the meet – so keep the dress simple and go for detail in your headwear.

Henley Royal Regatta

Founded in 1839, the Henley Royal Regatta is perhaps the most quintessentially British of all the Season's events. Men are expected to wear lounge suits or jackets/blazers with flannels, plus a tie or cravat. The dress code for women within the Steward's Enclosure highlights one of the most intriguing wardrobe rules that have resisted change. Women must wear a skirt or dress, the hemline of which should fall below the knee. No trousers, no jumpsuits, no miniskirts. In this respect, it is one of the strictest of dress codes and one that can present difficulties, as this length of skirt is not always easy to find. Even a maxi dress with a split will be refused entry by the eagle-eyed enclosure officials. It is customary, although not required, to wear a hat. It is less formal than Ascot in terms of the style of dress and hat – think floaty florals and summer straw hats, rather than formal skirt suits and statement headwear. It helps to look at the men's dress code first and then find the female equivalent (see page 13 for more information). Stiletto heels are always awkward

Henley Royal Regatta

on grass, so go for wedges or block-heeled sandals to give a more stable footing. There is no dress code within the Regatta Enclosure, but I would always recommend entering into the spirit of the occasion and adopting a similar look to that of the Steward's Enclosure. And if something is 'customary', then it is to be encouraged.

Wimbledon

Wimbledon is one of the four 'Grand Slams' of tennis – the most important tournaments for professional players. Most players will admit that Wimbledon is the top tournament and the one they dreamt of winning as a child. This has something to do with tradition, history and style. Respecting these principles makes the British carry off their seasonal events so well – not changing for the sake of change, and upholding certain traditions that are important to the attraction of the event (I did weep a little when the players' pre-/post-match bow to the Royal Box ended). But other stylish traditions are still alive and well: white sportswear is still the only colour allowed to be worn by players, for example. So strict is the 'all-white wear' rule that officials at the All England Club even enforce it for undergarments – heaven forbid that a coloured knicker ruffle should be flashed.

• For onlookers the dress code is thankfully more relaxed. For general ticket-holders there are no specific rules. It is advisable to wear loose-fitting clothes that are comfortable for sitting down all day – five-set matches can go on late into the evening. Bring a jacket or some form of cover-up if you are staying all day.

• In the debentures area the dress code has been relaxed in recent years to allow denim, but ripped jeans and trainers are still banned.

Wimbledon

• In the members area the dress code for men is lounge suit or tailored jacket, shirt, trousers and dress shoes, so ladies would be expected to match this, e.g. smart day dresses or smart two-piece outfits.

Glyndebourne

For a nation whose summers are as short as they are unpredictable, it is somewhat surprising that an outdoor black-tie Opera Festival should be held from May to August. Formal evening dress is customary at Glyndebourne (black tie/long or short dress). The dress

Glyndebourne

code is not enforced, but there are not many occasions these days that warrant the wearing of a long dress, so I would encourage such traditions to be followed. Dressing up here, as with most events, is a sign of respect to your host and performers. Yes, you can technically 'get away' with dressing down, but you wouldn't be entering into the spirit of the occasion, and are likely to stand out from the crowd in a negative way. Wraps or shawls are recommended, should the summer decide to go topsy-turvy, as is its wont. As it is an outdoor event, a lower block heel is recommended, rather than a spiky stiletto.

The Royal Caledonian Ball

The Royal Caledonian Ball is a Scottish dance and dinner held annually in May to benefit Scottish charities. It was first held in the 1840s as a private gathering hosted by the Duke and Duchess of Atholl for their Scottish friends who resided in London. Since 1930 the ball has been held at Grosvenor House Hotel on Park Lane; the ballroom of the Grosvenor is the largest in London and I know from experience that when Scots start to reel, you need as much space as possible! In terms of dress, ladies must wear floor-length gowns, and if partaking in the set reels, they must wear clan tartan sashes. Tiaras are optional but encouraged. Voluminous skirts are good for dancing and look good in colours that complement your tartan sash. The dress code for the ball is strictly enforced and entry is refused to those not appropriately dressed. Wear shoes in which you can comfortably dance, and make sure the hem of your dress is not too long – reels can be crowded affairs and long hemlines/trains are easily trodden on.

The Royal Caledonian Ball

Cowes Week

This prestigious sailing regatta on the Isle of Wight was first held in 1826 and takes place annually in early August. There isn't a formal dress code as such, but I would advise wearing lightweight clothing that can be layered according to the weather. Flat footwear is advisable – moccasins, espadrilles or deck shoes are the best options. In recent years, Cowes Week has featured a Ladies' Day (Tuesday). On this day, ladies are encouraged to wear nautical-themed clothing (navy-and-white stripes), with prizes awarded for the best outfits.

Cowes Week

Cartier International Polo

Held at the Guards Polo Club, Windsor, the Cartier
Queen's Cup polo tournament is held over three weeks
in May and June. The main event is, of course, the final,
held on the last Sunday of the tournament, the cup being
presented by HM The Queen, patron of the club. The
Queen's Cup final is usually a star-studded affair, so you
should dress to be seen. In the royal and members' areas
lounge suit is required. For all other areas, the dress code
is smart casual. For ladies, a smart summery dress is
appropriate, and shoes that are comfortable enough for
outdoors (and suitable for stomping in the divots!).

Cartier International Polo

The lady's maid's capsule wardrobe

Buy less, choose well, make it last.

VIVIENNE WESTWOOD

A capsule wardrobe is a small collection of essential garments that form the backbone of your wardrobe, regardless of what is currently in fashion. They are the garments that you are likely to hold on to for the longest, due to their timelessness and versatility, despite changing trends. You should therefore aim to choose these pieces well – look for colours and cuts that suit your shape and colouring – and buy the best quality that you can afford. Capsule classics should be seen as investment pieces that will stay in your wardrobe for years, maybe even decades, and are trusty garments that will never fail you.

If you have a good capsule wardrobe then you will find it a lot easier to dress and to maximise the number of outfits you can create from each garment. Creating a capsule wardrobe is also a great way of streamlining your wardrobe so that you can see what you actually wear the most. Sometimes it is easier to start from scratch – imagine you have moved home and you open the doors of an empty wardrobe. What are the 10 to 15 most wearable, versatile garments that you would unpack first before anything else? These should be your foundation capsule pieces around which you build the rest of your wardrobe.

Capsule garments should be from a neutral, coordinating colour palette. Black, grey, beige and white are the most neutral shades that are easy to mix and match with colours. Earthy, muted tones are also very good neutrals, e.g. khaki green, denim blue, navy blue, mocha brown,

nude pink – these shades are versatile additions to the
basic neutral palette. Listed below are my top choices for a
basic capsule winter wardrobe – they are all classic pieces
that won't go out of fashion. All these garments can be
mixed and matched together to create multiple different
outfits. The main point of having these classic pieces is
that any new colourful or patterned seasonal garment that
you introduce into your wardrobe will match up easily
with something from the classics already present. Each
capsule piece is also easy to dress up or down, depending
on whether you wear heels or flats.

Long-sleeved blouse

Blouses with a bit of neck detail like a 1980s-style pussy
bow, or Edwardian/Victoriana lace detail, are great as they
add a feminine touch to a plain blouse. Blouses can be
worn casually over jeans with a tailored jacket and flats,
or tucked into tailored trousers or a pencil skirt with heels
for a smarter look. Choose neutral shades, such as ivory
or blush pink.

Plain white shirt

The traditional collared white shirt is a must-have
wardrobe staple. As with the blouse it can be dressed
down with jeans and a cardigan, or dressed up with a
pencil skirt or tailored trousers. Lightweight shirts also
look good underneath crew-neck sweaters – the sharp
collar will smarten up the knitwear.

Winter capsule classics

Wool coat (black or neutral shade)

Long-line cardigan (black or neutral shade)

Denim jacket/denim shirt

Shirt dress

Crew-neck sweater (grey/neutral)

Long-sleeved blouse (ivory)

Tailored trousers (black/grey/navy)

Black blazer

Plain shirt (white)

High-neck jumper (black)

Black jeans

Pencil skirt (neutral/black)

A-line skirt (neutral/black)

Blue jeans

Crew-neck sweater

Crew-neck is more stylish than V-neck when it comes to knitwear. Choose fine yarns like merino wool if you are tucking the jumper into skirts, or loose fits and thicker wool for trouser or jean pairings. Grey may seem dull, but it is actually a very sophisticated colour and looks great when worn together with white and black or with bright skirts or trousers to neutralise the colour.

Long-line cardigan

Long-line cardigans are a good casual alternative to a coat or jacket inbetween seasons when you don't need the warmth of a winter coat. They look good worn over high-neck jumpers or blouses/shirts with skinny jeans, and can even be worn as a jumper-style dress with thick opaque tights and boots.

High-neck jumper

High-neck jumpers in black and neutral shades are great winter wardrobe staples that can be worn alone or underneath shift dresses, shirts or cardigans. If you are layering in this way, choose a fine merino wool knit.

Black jeans/blue jeans

The fashion for jeans is unlikely to fade like denim any time soon. Take a look at the high street and it's likely that most of the first ten people you see will be donning denim. Jeans have become an almost iconic wardrobe piece that have even crept into work and evening wear, due to the variety of cuts, colours and styles that are now available. Skinny jeans are everywhere now, but you may decide a slim leg or relaxed 'boyfriend' cut might be more flattering. I have a bit of a love–hate relationship with jeans and go through phases where I want to rebel against their mass following and ubiquitous presence, but I regularly come back to them for day-to-day casual outfits, for their ease of styling with tops and footwear. If you don't like the feeling of traditional denim against your skin, choose jeans made of soft denim – if they have a higher viscose or modal content, this will give them a silky soft feel, making them much comfier and easier to wear, and a particularly good option for travelling if you are sitting around airports and on long flights. You could also opt for 'jeggings' (a jean-leggings hybrid) that are much softer than pure denim. It is worth spending time finding the right pair of jeans and investing in good quality – they are probably the garment in your wardrobe that is worn the most, so the cost per wear will be low.

Tailored trousers

A workwear staple. Black is the most wearable colour, but navy blue or grey are good smart alternatives. If you are tucking a top into the trousers, then a high-waisted trouser with a built-in belt looks good. Cropped, 'cigarette' or ankle-grazing trousers are a flattering style, even in winter, as they show off the shoe to best effect. This style looks equally good with smart flat brogues or heels. The right shoes can really make or break an outfit, so you don't want to hide them under a hemline. They might not be the most attractive of garments, but knee-high tights (pop socks) are a wardrobe must that winterises the cropped trouser and keeps your ankles warm. Nothing is worse than a saggy sock, however, so invest in ones with a good grip. Marks and Sparks is a trusty supplier of all things undergarment related. They also have excellent seamless 'footsies' (a foot sock made of tight material that just grips the sole of the foot and isn't visible when wearing shoes), for when it is warm enough to bare your ankle to

the elements, but you still want to protect your feet from
blisters.

Wool coat

Black, grey or beige are the most versatile shades for
a coat that will match with every colour and style of
outfit, smart or casual. A camel coat is a chic and classic
wardrobe staple that will provide neutralising cover for
brightly coloured outfits, as well as complementing all
other shades of clothing. Winter white is a very good
smart alternative to black, especially for evening outfits.
For a coat that will take you from day to evening, work
to weekend, go for a longer-line, wrap-style coat with a
belted waist. The belt gives you the option of cinching in
the waist for a more fitted silhouette, and the length will
suit trousers and skirts. The coat should always match or
exceed the skirt length.

Black blazer

A black blazer is another essential for your smart–casual
wardrobe – worn with tailored separates or dressed down
with striped T-shirt and jeans, it instantly sharpens up any
outfit. I particularly like blazers that fasten with a single
gold button, rather than a black one, as it adds an air of
military/nautical chic.

Denim jacket/shirt

Denim jackets are useful between the seasons and will
match your outfit whatever its colour. A denim jacket can
dress down a tailored skirt or trousers and is also a good
casual cover-up for a floral dress in spring or summer.
Denim shirts are a good long-line alternative – and are also
useful to wear as a cover-up in spring and summer.

Pencil skirt

When skirts were the mainstay of women's wardrobes, hemlines would drop and rise in and out of fashion frequently. From the everyday A-line knee-length skirts of the 1940s to the pencil 'wiggle' or contrasting full 'prom'-style midis of the 1950s, the micro minis of the 1960s to the maxis popular in the 1970s to 1990s, each skirt style has been revisited in the twenty-first century, with midis very popular at the moment. All the other styles and lengths are still widely available, so it can be difficult to find the perfect skirt for all your wardrobe needs. For a skirt staple that is timeless and easy to wear, go for simple knee-length classic cuts, such as A-line or pencil. These styles tend to be the most flattering on all body shapes and will go with most tops.

Shirt dress

This is the most versatile style of dress due to its ability to transition from day to evening, work to weekend. A shirt dress can be dressed up with heels or dressed down with opaque tights and boots or flats. You can also add a belt to create a waistline, or layer it with a lightweight polo-neck or high-neck underneath in winter. As mentioned on page 18, shirt dresses are good garments to wear for smart-casual events.

Accessories

Accessories complete an outfit – even the plainest top and trousers can be transformed with the addition of the right scarf, bag and shoes. For footwear suitable for every outfit, start with classic neutral colours and styles, e.g. a plain leather or suede black court shoe, a classic black flat brogue, or brown leather Chelsea boots. Once you have the basics, you can afford to go off-piste a bit and get

coloured shoes too. But with these seven pairs of shoes –
two pairs of boots, two flats (one in tan/neutral and one
in black), two heels (one in tan/neutral and one in black),
plus white sneakers, you will always have appropriate
shoes to wear, no matter what colour or how smart/casual
your outfit is. Tan, camel and nude shades go with every
colour of clothing. For everyday shoes such as loafers and
ankle boots, invest in good quality leather rather than
cheap synthetic material, which will not allow your feet to
breathe and is likely to damage them if worn frequently.
Leather is a natural material so will stretch with your foot
and be much more comfortable. Choose handbags that
match your shoes – if you have one black and one neutral
bag, then you will always be perfectly colour coordinated.
Scarves are a great way of providing a flash of pattern
and colour to plain coats as well as warmth, so for winter
scarves, pick colours/patterns that complement your coats
and jackets – geometric patterns, like houndstooth or
tartan, are good classic options.

Apply the same idea to summer clothes with a lighter colour palette and lightweight fabrics. For spring/summer, it is a good idea to wear pieces that can be layered easily, to allow for fluctuations in temperature. Many of the pieces in the winter capsule wardrobe can still be worn in-between seasons too, e.g. the shirt dress, denim jacket and white shirt. Some summer dresses can also be winterised by adding opaque tights and a cardigan, or a slim-fitting polo-neck or high-neck underneath, depending on the style of the dress.

Wardrobe basics

Most people neglect the 'basics area' of their wardrobe, as it's much more fun to go shopping for sparkly shoes and fancy dresses than plain black or white tops. Wardrobe basics, such as plain tops and T-shirts, may seem boring, but they form the backbone of many outfits, so are an important part of your clothing collection. If you have a good selection of basic plain T-shirts/tops (short-sleeved, long-sleeved, sleeveless, strappy, long, cropped) in a variety of neutral colours (black or white being the most versatile), then you will always have something to match with a skirt or a pair of trousers – particularly if the skirt and trousers are patterned or textured and need something simple to balance the outfit.

Summer staples

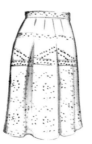

White cotton skirt

Blue shirt dress

Denim shorts

Black/white striped T-shirt

Tan handbag

Wedges (metallic shade)

White/neutral short-sleeved blouse

White/cream handbag

Flat sandals (tan/neutral)

Black sandals

Clutch bag
(metallic shade)

White linen or cotton cardigan

Flat espadrilles (white/neutral)

The top tee

The striped T-shirt is a favourite wardrobe staple and can be dressed down with jeans or up with a pencil skirt or black slim trousers and blazer. It can be worn on its own in summer or layered under a shirt or cardigan in winter. The stripes instantly smarten up the look of the T-shirt, and therefore the whole outfit. Black and white is the most versatile colour scheme, but other combinations such as red and white, or navy and white, are equally wearable. My wardrobe wouldn't be without at least three!

> *The duties of a lady's-maid towards her*
> *mistress being of a purely personal nature,*
> *propriety of demeanour and a well-informed*
> *mind are requisite qualities. The strictly technical*
> *knowledge required in the situation may be*
> *learnt in various ways; but no teaching will*
> *convey the delicate tact which proceeds from a*
> *pure mind, and the high sense of integrity which*
> *should characterise the slightest action where*
> *the interests and feelings of an employer are*
> *concerned.*
>
> *CASSELL'S HOUSEHOLD GUIDE*

A s a twenty-first-century lady's maid, I have had first-
hand experience of what it is like to be a modern-day
'servant', and to live with my colleagues and my employer
– a strange and unique existence that is sometimes hard
to explain. When working in such close proximity to your
employer a certain dependency develops, which is very
different from other working relationships. 'Living in'
the private household in which you work brings obvious
advantages: free accommodation, free food, no bills. But
there are also disadvantages: you spend most of your
time with either your boss or your colleagues; the world
outside your work dwindles; you are in danger of becoming
institutionalised. The job is certainly not for everyone; it
requires a specific set of skills and, more importantly, the
right temperament.

For all the downsides and the sacrifices that are
required by this particular profession, there has been an
equal number of upsides and bonuses. With live-in roles
there can be great camaraderie amongst staff. With travelling

A 1930s lady's maid attends her lady at her dressing table.

roles, I have had the opportunity to visit places I may never have visited independently and to stay in luxury hotels. But what was life like for ladies' maids in the past?

Cassell's Household Guide, published in 1869, described itself as 'a complete encyclopaedia of domestic and social economy and forming a guide to every department of practical life'. It was the go-to reference guide for all domestic workers in Victorian Britain. For a lady's maid there was an emphasis on the importance of the personal qualities that were required, as well as her proficiency in more practical skills, such as sewing or hairstyling. Such qualities were crucial because of the lady's maid's proximity to her employer. As her personal attendant, she would be in close contact with her several times a day – waking her up, assisting her to dress and undress, drawing her bath. Being a constant presence in her lady's domain, she would perhaps overhear private conversations, or indeed even become a confidante. Ladies' maids were expected to be more educated than housemaids and trusted to keep their mistresses' secrets and not to betray them by gossiping with other below-stairs staff.

Styling a summer holiday wardrobe

I get ideas about what's essential when packing my suitcase.

DIANE VON FURSTENBERG

Packing for a holiday can present decision anxiety in even the most seasoned of travellers. While it can be tempting to force your entire wardrobe and accessories collection into one suitcase and leave decision-making until you reach your destination, I strongly advise against this. You will weigh down your suitcase unnecessarily, half the clothes won't be worn and you'll just have more work to do unpacking and packing again – valuable time taken out of your holiday. If you are organised and selective, you can still have plenty of outfits to wear without your suitcase bursting at the seams. The key to a light suitcase is a bit of pre-holiday outfit planning and prioritising pieces that can be worn multiple ways.

Top tips for styling your summer holiday wardrobe

• Lay out all of the clothes that you could take with you – as many as you want at this stage. It will help you to see what you have and make the styling process easier.
• Select outfits according to the length of your holiday. For a one-week holiday select one day outfit and one evening outfit for each day of the holiday. If it is an extended trip, then there will be repeat wears. Avoid too many 'statement one-piece outfits', i.e. patterned/beaded dresses, as it is likely you will only wear these once.
• Separates are good for multiple wears, e.g. a patterned

skirt or pair of trousers that can be dressed up or down
with different plain tops and different accessories. Pick out
one separate and see how many different looks you can
create with it by dressing it up and down and mixing and
matching with your other garments.

• Don't allow anything to enter your suitcase unless you
have already styled it into an outfit – this is the most
important tip in order to avoid over-packing. If you haven't
got anything to wear with a garment at this stage, you're
not going to wear it on holiday.

• Limit your shoes to the following: one pair of flip-flops,
one or two pairs of flat sandals, one pair of comfortable
neutral flats for walking, e.g. espadrilles or moccasins,

and one pair of gold or silver flat sandals for evening.
Shoes take up a lot of space in your suitcase, so it's really
important to be selective here. If you want to take heels,
heeled wedges are a better choice for sunny destinations.
Neutral colours, such as white, beige, tan and metallic, are
ideal for summer – they will go with all your outfits.
• Select a couple of neutral bags – white/tan/metallic – that
match the shoes you've selected.

Let's imagine you have a holiday to a hot destination such
as Abu Dhabi coming up. On the left I have pictured a pair
of cool and elegant grey/white patterned harem trousers
and selected some other pieces to match with these
trousers to create a day look: a simple, round-necked
tank top, white espadrille flats and a white linen cardigan.
These pieces are all very versatile and could be matched
with lots of other garments for multiple wears. As there is
a lot of white you can afford to add some colour in your
accessories. Turquoise or metallic jewellery looks great
with white (and a sun-tan!).

For evening, the same trousers can be worn with a
silver, sequined shift top, silver wedges and matching
metallic clutch. For another evening look, the silver top
could be worn again with the silver wedges and a pair of
white trousers. The silver wedges and clutch will go with
any brightly coloured outfits, too. Try and get at least two
wears out of each piece that you pack. See Pack like a Pro
on page 110 for further tips on packing your suitcase.

What to wear to Buckingham Palace

The Queen and other members of the royal family host numerous lunches, dinners and receptions at Buckingham Palace throughout the year in association with charities and organisations of which they are patrons, or to recognise sporting achievements. All invitees to events will receive an invitation stating the dress code expected. Lunches and day or evening drinks receptions are likely to be lounge suit; dinners will be either lounge suit or black tie. Other, more formal events include State banquets, held a couple of times a year for visiting Heads of State (white tie); the Diplomatic Reception, held annually and attended by ambassadors and diplomats (white tie or national dress); investitures (morning suit); and garden parties (morning suit). If you are lucky enough to be invited to such an event, you will want to spend time planning your outfit in advance and be appropriately attired, so that when the day comes around you can enjoy the special occasion without fretting about your outfit.

Royal garden parties

Invitations to royal garden parties will state 'Morning Dress or Uniform or Lounge Suit'. Lounge suit attire is therefore suitable (i.e. hats are not obligatory), but I would advise dressing more formally and donning a headpiece. The Queen hosts garden parties in the gardens of Buckingham Palace (and one in Holyrood) from May to July. Dress in formal daywear as if you were going to a summer wedding or Ascot (see page 23). The event will obviously be outdoors on grass and you may have to spend some time

Royal garden party

queuing at the gates, so wear comfortable shoes. National dress and military uniform can be worn, if appropriate.

Investitures

Investiture outfits – winter and summer

An investiture is the ceremony where members of the public who have been awarded honours (such as MBEs or knighthoods) receive the physical insignia from the Queen (or other members of the royal family). Around 1,250 members of the public are honoured each year, for outstanding achievements in public life, personal bravery and services to the UK. The list of recipients is announced twice yearly (New Year's Day and HM's Birthday), but the actual ceremonies take place throughout the year, within the ballroom of Buckingham Palace or the Waterloo chamber at Windsor Castle. As with a royal garden party, the dress code for investitures is 'Morning Dress or Uniform or Lounge Suit'.

Dress appropriately for the time of year and for an indoor event. Most ladies receiving awards wear a hat, but bear in mind that it is an indoor ceremony, so a small, simple hat/headpiece is more appropriate than an extravagant 'Ladies' Day' number. See Appendix I for suggestions of milliners that are good for discreet, beret-style hats. You will be given a special pin to wear on your top so that your insignia can be easily hooked on to your clothing, so it's probably good to pick a strong fabric to support your shiny medal! In winter it is advisable to wear a long-sleeved dress, suit, or dress coat, for when you go outside for photos. Sensible heels in which you can walk comfortably are a good idea too – the walk towards the Queen will seem even longer if you are in four-inch stilettos.

Investitures

Dress like a princess

Our life dictates a certain kind of wardrobe.

GRACE KELLY

Towards the end of the twentieth century, there was one royal princess notable for her style – Diana, Princess of Wales. Who could forget the midnight blue Victor Edelstein gown that she wore to dance with John Travolta at the White House in 1985. This simple but striking off-the-shoulder evening dress was one of 79 gowns chosen by Diana to be auctioned for charity in the 1997 Christie's sale 'Dresses' just two months before her untimely death. The 'Travolta' dress was later re-sold at auction in 2013, purchased by a British gentleman as a surprise for his wife, for the princely sum of £240,000. The 1980s and 1990s were not great fashion decades, when wearing boxy

Top tips for regal wardrobes

• Accessories. Royal ladies have a much larger formal wardrobe than most women and they are often expected to wear a new outfit to each event. This is made easier by having neutral accessories – the Queen's shoes and handbag rarely change from black despite the kaleidoscope of colour that you will see in her dress. Similarly, the Duchess of Cambridge is often seen with neutral court shoes and matching clutch. If you have trusty neutral accessories then shopping and dressing for formal events will be much easier.

• Sleeve length. Dresses available in the summer are often of the sleeveless variety. Royal ladies usually have their upper arms covered at formal day events – if the dress is sleeveless, then a matching dress coat or jacket is often worn. A more common look for the younger royals is to forgo the coat and wear a dress with sleeves – which are usually three-quarter length or long.

• Jewellery. You can't go wrong with pearls, a timeless addition to every lady's jewellery box – they instantly add a touch of chic to any outfit. Discreet jewelled studs, or jewelled tear-drop earrings, are also very elegant. Save the flashy diamonds for evening events.

suits, neon brights and that magical 'meringue' wedding dress, Diana's personal style shone through – a sign of a true style icon. And, as exemplified by the intricately embroidered and expertly cut Catherine Walker gowns of the 1990s, Diana rarely put a style foot wrong.

The twenty-first century has brought a new wave of young and stylish European royals – most notably Mary, Crown Princess of Denmark, Queen Letizia of Spain and Britain's own Duchess of Cambridge. The newest addition to the British Royal family, Meghan Markle, the Duchess of Sussex, has a noticeably fresher, more modern style. Like Kate, everything Meghan wears is scrutinised and sells out within hours – for this reason, Kate and Meghan are currently the ladies most designers dream of wearing their designs. Royal ladies dress a certain way and follow a traditional dress code etiquette, such as hats always being worn for formal day events. The look is usually elegant and modest: miniskirts and plunge necklines are not often seen, for example. It is clear that Royals have to toe the line between dressing in a way that respects their title and public role while not being seen to be spending outrageous amounts of money on designer fashion. Diplomatic dressing is often seen; for example, on foreign trips they will pay tribute to fashion designers of their host country by wearing outfits from local designers, which inevitably boosts sales there and thus, implicitly, relations between the countries. The Duchess of Cambridge, in particular, is noted for wearing both high-street and high-end clothing, bringing publicity and business to the British fashion industry across the price spectrum.

WHAT IS A LADY'S MAID?

The following is a 1935 advertisement for the position of lady's maid to Mrs Miranda Bouchard of Chester Square, Belgravia. The job was secured by 17-year-old Anwyn Moyle and remembered in her memoir, *Her Ladyship's Girl: A Maid's Life in London*.

> *WANTED: lady's maid who is modest in person and manner and maintains the strictest sense of honour. Trust is a must. She will read and speak pleasantly; and have neat, legible handwriting. Preferably skilled in plain work (darning stockings, mending linen). Fastidious and discreet, the ideal candidate will have the ability to plait muslin in addition to performing daily duties in a timely manner. Experience desirable. References essential.*

A lady's maid is a close female attendant, assistant and sometimes confidante to the lady of the house, responsible for the care and management of all the lady's personal belongings. The duties of the role vary depending on the personal requirements of the lady, but traditionally a lady's maid's primary function is to be in charge of her mistress's wardrobe and to attend to her throughout the day. Traditional duties would include some or all of the following: laying out outfits several times a day; assisting with dressing, styling hair and make-up; sewing and mending clothing; hand-washing and pressing of garments; tidying the bedroom and dressing room, including preparing the dressing table with make-up/creams; packing luggage for travel; personal shopping; care of accessories, including jewellery, handbags, shoes and furs; taking calling trays/

breakfast trays; and running baths. Ladies' maids might also be expected to keep a detailed inventory of clothing and outfits worn to specific functions, advise her lady on style and the latest fashions, source new outfits from designers and retailers, and accompany her lady on outings as a sort of chaperone. So it was a very unique role amongst the servants of the house – and one that required discretion, intelligence, trust and loyalty.

Position in the household

Among the female staff of the house in Victorian and Edwardian times, the head housekeeper would be the most senior servant, but the lady's maid would have closer daily contact with the lady of the house and so would be under the direction of her lady rather than the housekeeper. All the other female staff (laundry maids and housemaids) would be under the management of the housekeeper and head butler. For this reason, the lady's maid would often be somewhat isolated from other staff members – not regarded as equal to the housekeeper and head butler, but senior to the housemaids and laundry maids. The lady's maid would often take her meals with the housekeeper and butler and would have junior servants waiting on her.

The decline of the lady's maid

Although not common in the twenty-first century, there are still a few households in Britain that employ ladies' maids – mainly royal households (where they are known as 'dressers') and other wealthy families with extensive wardrobes who choose to run their house with a more traditional staff hierarchy. In the nineteenth and early-twentieth centuries, it was fairly common for all aristocratic English ladies to employ a lady's maid amongst their large retinue of staff. After the Second World War, domestic service as a choice for British workers went into decline, employers began to streamline their household staff in order to cut costs, and so the more specialised duties and personal service of a lady's maid would have merged with the housemaids' roles within most of these households. These days, the role will either merge with that of a housekeeper or that of a personal assistant. Or, a lady might enlist the services of stylists, beauticians and hairdressers, whose work was also once taken on by the multi-skilled lady's maid. The job title may be a dying breed, but the duties of a lady's maid still exist, even if they are fulfilled by other means.

A *Punch* cartoon from 1895 shows a lady's maid travelling with her employer. The caption pokes fun at the huge number of 'necessities' the maid has to remember to pack – everything from a pencil case to ice skates.

Dressing for an interview

While it is true that one should not judge a book by its cover, it is also true that first impressions count. This is particularly important in the case of dressing for an interview, when your interviewer will form an impression of you within seconds based on your appearance.

You have a small window of time to present yourself and impress your interviewer. Whether or not your outfit is 'fashionable' is not so important (unless you are interviewing for a fashion-related job). What is important is wearing something clean, smart and not too distracting in any way. While you are there to prove your ability to do the job, your impact will be hindered if you wear anything that distracts from what you are saying. Dressing appropriately for an interview is not only important in terms of giving a good impression on the day – if you are going to be representing a company to its clients, the employer will want to see that you will look the part.

Not all interviews require you to don a sharp suit – a basic rule is to consider what you would wear day to day if you were in the job, and then notch it up a bit in the style stakes. Having said that, no one is going to criticise you for wearing a suit if you want to, it will show that you are keen to make a good first impression, which is the most important thing.

Top tips for dressing to impress

• **Style.** If opting for a suit, choose a fabric suitable for daytime (no velvet or satin). Skirts should be a decent knee-length. A sharp white shirt (make sure the collar is clean and pressed) or plain neutral blouse underneath the jacket is the best option top-wise, unless your suit jacket is very fitted, in which case you may need just a plain T-shirt/top underneath. An alternative option to the suit is a long-sleeved shift dress – classic, elegant and smart. Crew necklines are the best style – avoid any décolletage-revealing numbers. Check your outfit before you leave for stray dog hairs or loose buttons, and make sure everything is pressed. No jeans. Even if you are interviewing for a trendy advertising agency, where anything goes clothes-wise day to day. Jeans are generally a bad idea if you want to be taken seriously in an interview.

• **Colour.** If wearing a suit, choose classic dark colours – black, navy or grey. In the summer, paler or pastel colours are acceptable. Avoid bright colours or garish patterns, which will be too distracting.

• **Jewellery.** As with colour, avoid any jewellery that is too distracting, such as dangly earrings or massive pendants. Simple stud earrings are the safest choice, and a necklace that isn't too glaring.

• **Shoes.** Wear smart and comfortable polished shoes – heels look good with skirts and trousers and are appropriate up to a certain height (no more than 3in/7.5cm), but make sure you can comfortably wear them and choose a classic colour that matches the outfit. I once saw a prospective nanny arriving for an interview wearing high-heeled gold stilettos. Needless to say, she did not get the job. Your outfit should be appropriate for your prospective job – and no one wears stilettos when they're running around after children. Trainers are also a no-no.

• **Bag.** Match the colour of your bag with your shoes. A large business-style top-handle bag is the best choice if you are wearing a suit – even if you don't have anything in it besides your Rescue Remedy and your train fare home.

Cultural clothing – modest fashion

Modesty is the highest elegance.

COCO CHANEL

Dress and religion

In 2014, the Qatar Islamic Cultural Centre launched a
'Reflect Your Respect' campaign on social media and via
leaflets in the country, stating 'When you are in Qatar,
you are one of us'. Its aim was to get visitors to attire
themselves accordingly. As with a formal dress code for an
event, dressing appropriately abroad is a sign of respect
to your host. Some people find packing for trips difficult
at the best of times, but if a work trip or holiday takes
you to the Middle East, you may find it challenging to find
appropriate garments in your wardrobe. It is essential
that you do a bit of homework on what to wear to your
destination in order not to cause offence to the locals, or
possibly even risk arrest. Some Middle Eastern countries
are more relaxed than others – the stricter the dress code
for the locals, the more you should emulate their dress,
in order to respect their customs and religion. They will
respect you for it in return.

In most Muslim countries it is advisable for female
visitors to adopt a 'modest' wardrobe when in public
places (e.g. shopping malls, markets and public areas of
hotels). Modest is usually defined as the wearing of loose-
fitting clothing that covers at least the upper legs to the
knee and the upper arms. If you are visiting a religious
place, such as a mosque, or if you are travelling during
the holy month of Ramadan, then modesty is even more

important. Most mosques and Catholic churches will have dress codes posted outside the building to display what is and isn't permitted. Sleeveless tops, shorts and short skirts are not allowed in for example. Mosques will require ladies to wear a headscarf and the removal of shoes. Many mosques and Christian cathedrals will provide robes or scarves at the door for tourists who don't arrive appropriately dressed.

Aside from the religious and cultural considerations, many Middle Eastern countries have a hot climate for much of the year, so loose clothing is advisable from a comfort point of view too, as it will keep you cool; plus, if you cover up, you will be protected from the sun's harmful rays when out and about. Breathable natural fabrics, such as cotton, linen and silk, are the best options for hot climates. Indoor public places will always be air-conditioned to the max, so it isn't necessary to wear skimpy clothing in order to keep cool. See Appendix I for my stockists of appropriate Muslim and heatwave-friendly fashion.

Modest dressing doesn't have to be restricted to visiting Muslim countries – many people choose to dress more conservatively in European countries, regardless of their religious beliefs. There has been a resurgence in modest clothing on the catwalk in recent years, resulting in looser silhouettes, higher necklines and lower hemlines being found much more frequently on the high street. This is most noticeable with skirt hemlines – midi skirts are now much more widely available and popular. Jumpsuits are a particularly trendy and elegant option for Muslim-friendly day and evening wear as they tend to be loosely fitted. Summer shirt dresses, palazzo pants and midi skirts and dresses are other good fashionable additions to your modest wardrobe. With a bit of research and effort, it is perfectly possible to wear modest clothing and not appear dowdy: loose-fitting doesn't have to be baggy – it just shouldn't be skintight (body-con is a definite no-no), so with the right pieces, 'modest' outfits can look incredibly stylish and elegant. Style has never been about showing off your figure – it's about wearing clothes well.

What to wear – modest dress

✓	✗
Long-sleeved loose tops – cotton and linen fabrics are best in hot climates	Strapless tops
Loose-fitting trousers, e.g. palazzo pants	Sleeveless tops (unless you wear with a cardigan)
Round or high necklines	Crop tops
Jumpsuits	Short dresses
Long, loose-fitting skirts; midi or maxi are best	Deep V-necklines
Tunics and kaftans	Spaghetti straps
Long-sleeved cardigans – loose with linen content are a good cover-up for sleeveless tops	Leggings – only advisable if worn with a long tunic top
A light scarf if visiting mosques	Tight, fitted dresses, e.g. body-con
Capri pants provide good coverage for legs while still keeping you cool	Shorts
Harem trousers	Mini skirts
	Tight skinny or ripped jeans
	Translucent/transparent clothing – underwear should not be visible
	Swimwear (away from the pool/beach)

Styling scarves

When I wear a silk scarf I feel so definitely like a woman, a beautiful woman.

AUDREY HEPBURN

Scarves are a great way to accessorise an outfit with a flash of colour. Silk patterned scarves, in particular, can add an eye-catching touch of elegance and style to an otherwise plain outfit. Silk scarves were historically and famously worn to protect hairdos from the wind; style icons such as Audrey Hepburn and Grace Kelly were notable devotees of this look, popular in the 1950s. Kelly even fashioned one into a sling for her broken arm in 1959. The Queen is one of the few who are still loyal to the headscarf these days, but silk scarves remain a very popular fashion accessory when worn around the neck.

Square scarves

The classic silk scarf can be tied many different ways to achieve different looks. A silk scarf oozes style – what could be more elegant than adding a sliver of silk about your neck? Whether worn around the head, neck or handbag, this silk square is a timeless fashion accessory.

Cowboy

The easiest way to wear a square scarf is the 'cowboy'.
Fold the square in half to form a triangle. Roll the straight
end over slightly, to create more of a collar around the
neck and shorten the size of the triangle. Pass the triangle
around the neck with the V pointing towards the front,
then cross the two ends over and bring towards the front.
A variation is achieved by tying the two ends in a knot at
the back of the triangle or at the front. Move the knot to
either side or leave at the front, according to preference.

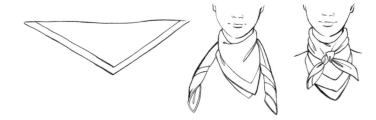

Double knot

A classic, Parisian chic look. Fold the square into a narrow
strip, as shown below, and then wrap the strip around the
neck and tie in a double knot at one side. For a shorter
bow, wrap the scarf around the neck twice before tying.

Classic tie

A simple, classic look that particularly complements plain tailored suits. Triangle-fold the square and then continue to fold to create the narrow strip. Pass around the neck, leaving one end longer than the other. Tie a loose knot in the middle of the longer end. Pull the other length through the knot and then tighten the knot slightly, so that it sits in the middle of the tie.

Crossed turban

You can even wear your scarf as a headband – fold as above and then pass the strip across the back of the head, bringing the two ends up to the top. Cross over and tie in a knot at the back of the neck. To accessorise a bun, cross the strip around the bun several times and tie in a double knot at the front.

Skinny scarves

These scarves can be tied around the neck and head, as with square scarves, and can also be used to accessorise a handbag – wrap tightly around the handle and tie in a knot at each end.

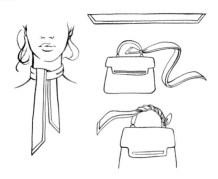

Long scarves (rectangular)

The long scarf is probably the most common and popular shape these days and comes in a variety of weaves/knit thicknesses. I prefer a lightweight scarf even in the depths of winter – when bunched up, scarves with a fine weave still provide the warmth you need around your neck outside, without stifling you when you walk into a heated building. They are also soft on the skin, whereas some thicker, woollen scarves can be scratchy. There are numerous ways of tying this style of scarf, including these favourites.

Neck loop

This style forms a nice neat loop around the neck without any ends hanging down. Loop the scarf around the neck once, leaving one end slightly longer than the other. Wrap the longer end around the back again, tucking the end into the neck loop to secure. Wrap the shorter end around the front and tuck in to secure.

Neck loop with front knot

In this variation, drape the scarf around the neck leaving one end slightly longer than the other. Pass the longer end around the neck and bring back to the front. Form a loose knot with the two ends at the front. Rearrange the neck loop so that it covers the knot, if desired.

Blanket scarves

Blanket scarves are over-sized scarves. Many people can be a little overwhelmed (literally) by the volume of their fabric. Some of them can be the size of a picnic blanket, so can look a little cumbersome and bulky when wrapped around the neck. But if folded and tied correctly, you should still be able to see above the layers! They do undeniably provide snug-as-a-bug warmth around the neck and face in very cold climates. Because of the volume of fabric, they give a textured look that appears different every time you wear them. Patterned styles are definitely better than plain, in order to break up the bulk of fabric with some variations in colour. There are four basic ways of draping a blanket scarf, with variations.

Cowboy (three variations)

Start by making a triangle fold. To give more variation
in the layers of the scarf, fold so that the triangle is not
precisely aligned. Pass around your neck as in the cowboy
style (as illustrated with the silk square on p. 64). Arrange
the folds of the fabric as desired. The ends can be left
loose or, to reduce the bulk of the fabric, tie or tuck
behind the front triangle, or tie the ends in front.

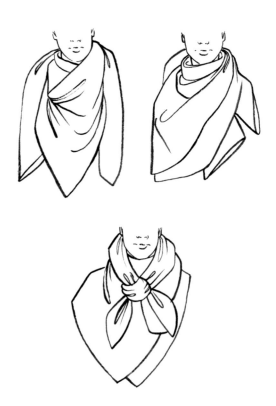

Long loop

Start with a triangle fold and then fold from the straight
side towards the point until you have a long narrow strip
– so, effectively, you have turned it into a long rectangular
scarf. Holding the centre point with one hand and the two
ends with the other, pass around the neck. Bring either
one or both ends through the loop. This look is good for
creating lots of texture – tweak the folds until you have the
desired look.

Infinity loop

Start with the long strip as above, and tie the ends
together in a double knot. Loop around the neck twice for
a snug, neck-warming fit.

Shawl

The blanket scarf can be styled into a shawl/poncho in place of a jacket – triangle fold and drape around the shoulders. Fold slightly at the neck to create a small collar. This style can be secured with a belt or brooch, if desired.

LADIES' MAIDS AND THE NATIONAL TRUST

So there I was, I'd reached the top rung of the ladder for my kind of job. What I had to do was to stay there. It wasn't to prove easy and I swayed about a lot in the earlier years. Eventually I learnt to be an acrobat.

ROSINA HARRISON, LADY'S MAID TO LADY ASTOR AT CLIVEDEN, 1929–64

Rosina Harrison's memoir, *The Lady's Maid: My Life in Service*, first published in 1975, gives us a first-hand account of what life was really like as a lady's maid in Great Britain in the first half of the twentieth century. Rosina (known as Rose) was a lady's maid to Nancy, Lady Astor – wife of fellow American expat Lord Waldorf Astor, and the first female MP to have a seat in parliament in the UK. Their country home was Cliveden in Buckinghamshire, which was to be Rose's home too, and place of work, for the 35 years of service that she gave to Lady Astor.

Rose, a country girl from Yorkshire, expressed a desire to travel from a young age – it was this that perhaps led her in the direction of becoming a lady's maid, as she was aware that the role often involved travel; ladies' maids were expected to accompany their employers on any trips that they made, both at home and abroad. This gave the role considerable appeal to many ambitious servants of the time. Only the closest servant attendants (the female lady's maid and the male valet) would have this opportunity for travel; the rest of the domestic staff would be permanently based in their employer's residence. So, if you were a domestic servant – destined for a life of drudgery – travel was certainly a form of escape and a break with routine; an opportunity to see places that you wouldn't otherwise visit.

Rose's mother knew that if this was her daughter's goal, she needed to ensure that she became more educated than most of the young girls her age, in order to be eligible to apply for this more senior servant role. She therefore stayed in school until the age of 16 (rather than the usual leaving age of 14), she learned dressmaking as an apprentice for two years and took French lessons.

At the age of 18 Rose acquired her first job as a junior lady's maid to the daughters of Lady Irene Tufton, based in Mayfair. Junior ladies' maids worked for the daughters of the lady of the house, so this was ideal training for Rose's future role working for Lady Astor. Here she learned how to iron different fabrics, how to remove stains, make undergarments, how to pack for trips, as well as build up experience in being a close attendant to her employer: dressing, chaperoning, taking calling trays, etc. Rose describes the household as being a 'busy but happy lot' and she enjoyed the bustle of London, in contrast to her country roots. She was, however, aware of the limitations of domestic service, even in her more senior and varied role; she couldn't rely on time off and there was a 10 p.m. curfew, so it was difficult to make her own plans. 'There was no status in service,' Rose remembers, 'you were a nobody, marriage was the only way out of it.'

Rose worked for the Tufton ladies for four years before deciding she wanted a change of scenery, and more money. Her next role was working for Lady Cranbourne as a fully-fledged lady's maid. This role was also based in London but it gave her the opportunity to fulfil her ambition to travel. While with Lady Cranbourne, Rose visited Eze and Antibes in the South of France, Paris and Rome. Rose was aware that ladies' maids were judged by the way their employers were dressed – they became a walking advertisement for the lady's maid's skills in the job. Rose visited fashion shows with Lady Cranbourne and put her dressmaking skills to good use by making garments influenced by what she saw.

Rose's first introduction to Cliveden came during this time. Lady Cranbourne was a friend of Lady Astor and would stay at Cliveden during Ascot. After five years with Lady Cranbourne, Rose was still earning only £24 per year – the same as her income with the Tuftons. Pay rises were not offered, so the only way she could get an increase in salary was to change employers. Rose felt this was important so that she could send more money home to support her mother. As a well-established lady's maid, Rose didn't feel the need to go through an employment agency, so she put the word out amongst the service grapevine that she was looking for a new role. In 1928, while spending Ascot at Cliveden as usual, Rose became aware of a vacancy working for Lady Astor's daughter. It was a step back, as it wasn't for the lady of the house, but the salary was £60 per year – more than double her previous salary – so she needed little persuasion.

After a short period working for Miss Wissie, Lady Astor's daughter, Rose was promoted to work for Lady Astor herself, following the departure of her own lady's maid. Rose noted how the duties of the job itself were not challenging, but her mistress sometimes could be: 'Dressing her wasn't difficult; what was impossible was to attempt to keep up with her quicksilver mind.' Perhaps this explains the run of unsuitable maids that left prior to Rose taking up the position – one even did a 'moonlight flit' – disappearing in the night without even collecting her wages. But with Rose, it seems Lady Astor had met her match in temperament, and Rose at least attempted to give as good as she got. Rose had the strength of character not to be fazed by the temperament of Lady Astor, nor to take criticism personally – characteristics that stood her in good stead to withstand 35 years in her service.

Servant bell at Cliveden, linking the servant hall with the Lady's Maid's bedroom.

PART II
WARDROBE
ORGANISATION

The wardrobe space

She thinks she's found a magical land ...
In the upstairs wardrobe.

THE LION, THE WITCH AND THE WARDROBE, C.S. LEWIS

Unless you have the luxury of a lady's maid at your beck and call, you may find chaos creeping into your wardrobe quicker than the time it takes for a clothes moth to have breakfast, lunch and dinner in your knitwear drawer. If you want to keep your clothes and accessories visible, accessible and in the best condition, the first thing you need to consider is how to organise and store them properly within your wardrobe space. Many of the wardrobes I have worked with have been 'walk-in' wardrobes or dressing rooms, where the entire room stores and displays clothing and accessories. Sometimes I have entered these spaces wondering if I will ever escape,

hoping I might be transported into a Narnia world full of snow and Turkish delight! You may not have the luxury of a walk-in wardrobe on this scale, but it is still possible to be creative and inventive with the space you have in order to maximise storage possibilities and to display your clothes and accessories to best effect, so that each garment can be viewed and located easily.

Bespoke wardrobes

Bespoke wardrobes are good because they can be fitted into very small bedrooms and dressing rooms, or even under-stairs cupboards, and they allow you to design the storage space according to the size of the room and the type of garments to be stored. A section of the room wall-to-wall becomes the wardrobe so that storage space can be maximised. When designing the wardrobe, it is especially important to exploit the vertical space – right up to the ceiling. Higher shelves are better than no shelves; and these can be used for items not in regular use, such as occasion hats, special shoes or off-season chunky knits. Bespoke wardrobes don't have to be expensive – many department stores offer made-to-measure wardrobe solutions that can be built to suit your space and clothing needs (see Appendix I for some suggestions). Sliding doors are a good space-saving option to eliminate the area needed for wardrobe doors to open, and they can also double up as full-length mirrors in which to view your perfectly styled outfits.

With a bespoke wardrobe, it is advisable to have adjustable hanging rails and shelves within the wardrobe to allow for moving your things around and to ensure each garment has enough space. Shorter items, such as shirts and tops, trousers and skirts, can be hung on rails one above the other to utilise the full height of the wardrobe, whereas long dresses will need to be hung on one high rail so that they hang freely without getting crumpled. Shelving units can be used to display items such as bags, shoes and folded clothing. When designing your wardrobe space or buying storage solutions, consider what sort of wardrobe space would best suit you. If you have a lot of suits and dresses you may prefer to have more hanging space rather than shelves; or perhaps you have a lot of knitwear and bags, in which case shelving units would work better for you. Shallow drawers are better than deeper ones for displaying items such as underwear, socks, nightwear and also accessories, such as jewellery, gloves and belts, for ease of access and so that each item can be viewed properly and located quickly.

Storage solutions

If you find you still don't have quite enough space for all of your clothing and accessories, there are additional storage solutions you can employ, both within the wardrobe itself and outside it. If you have limited storage space, it will be even more important to follow the guide within the Cleanse your Closet section on page 82 and to keep control of the size, organisation and content of your clothing collection.

• **Portable hanging rails** are practical and economical if you need extra hanging space. You can buy adjustable portable rails, or decorative ones to fit in with the style of the room as a more permanent fixture, if you have the space. The downside of these is that your clothing will be exposed to dust, so make sure you only use clothing rails for everyday clothing that is worn and washed regularly.

- **A hanging shoe organiser** can be fixed over a hanging rail to allow you to store multiple pairs of shoes. They are particularly good for flat and casual shoes. You could also store scarves, belts and other accessories here.
- **A multi-hook rail** can be fixed over the backs of doors for hanging coats and bags. Coats are the bulkiest of garments, so if you have space for a separate wardrobe or hook rail in a hallway, this will free up some space in your main wardrobe. These hooks are okay for some resilient waterproofs or towelling dressing gowns, but try not to hang coats and jackets by the loop at their neck for too long – garments should be supported by hangers, where possible, to prevent damage to the fabric.
- **Out-of-season clothing** can be stored on top of the wardrobe or outside of the main wardrobe, to free up space for clothing in wear during the current season. This depends on your climate – in England it is hard to know when summer is coming and how long it will last, and you'll find many of your clothes will cross seasons, but items such as bulky knitwear take up a lot of space and won't be needed for several months of the year, even in England. Place in garment storage boxes in a spare room, on top of your wardrobe or in under-bed storage bags. Be sure that any storage boxes and bags that you use are appropriate for clothing – they should be breathable and not plastic. See Seasonal Storage on page 109 for tips on how to correctly store off-season clothing.
- **Baskets or boxes** could be placed on higher shelves within the wardrobe to keep together bulkier accessories that are awkward to store elsewhere, such as belts, bags and flip-flops.

Cleanse your closet

In most women's lives, everything, even the greatest sorrow, comes down to a question of 'I haven't got a thing to wear'.

THE GUERMANTES WAY, MARCEL PROUST

Deciding what to wear each day is made much easier if you have an ordered closet. The much-heard sartorial refrain 'I have nothing to wear' is often due to clothing clutter – it is hard to create an outfit if you cannot easily locate one. The feeling of having a lot of clothes and yet nothing to wear is partly due to poor organisation within the wardrobe and partly due to buying items that either don't suit you or don't suit your existing clothes. One of the main reasons people have too many clothes that they don't wear is because they buy separates (i.e. tops, trousers and skirts) without thinking how they fit in to their current wardrobe, or what they are going to wear with them. So, the pretty top that seduced you in the magazine or shop languishes in the wardrobe never seeing the light of day. To prevent this mistake, whenever you buy a new top/skirt/pair of trousers, ask yourself what garment in your current wardrobe you would wear it with. If there isn't anything, the likelihood is that it will remain unworn.

Another common reason for clothes remaining unworn, with their tags still on, is a SALE purchase. People tend to lose all sense of reason when faced with a sale rack with signs screaming '50 per cent off'. I know what it is like to lose all rationale when faced with sale signs in the footwear department. I find a quick turn around haberdashery helps to ease the palpitations. Yes, it might well be a bargain. Yes, you've done very well to find the garment, and in your size too. But ask yourself whether you would have been attracted to the item in the first place without the sale tag; if the answer is no, then don't buy it. Make sensible choices when shopping for clothes and try to resist impulse buying. Or if you cannot resist, try not to make a habit of it – everyone is allowed a flight of fancy now and then.

Convert clothing chaos into calm

Have nothing in your house that you do not know to be useful or believe to be beautiful.

WILLIAM MORRIS

Marie Kondo, decluttering expert and author of *The Life-Changing Magic of Tidying Up: The Japanese Art of Decluttering and Organizing*, puts Morris's famous sentiment even more simply – she encourages people to eliminate any possessions that don't 'spark joy'.

Clutter is definitely something to avoid, especially within the wardrobe. Ladies who employ a lady's maid are evidently in need of someone full-time to impart some order on to the chaos that can become a woman's wardrobe. But whatever the size of your clothing collection, it is still important to adopt a little organisation and appropriate decision-making in order to get the best out of it. A UK YouGov survey (commissioned by Marks & Spencer in 2012) revealed that there are around 2.4 billion pieces of clothing lying unworn per year in the UK, cluttering up wardrobes across the land. This equates to approximately 46 per cent of the national wardrobe. A similar survey in 2017 conducted by Weight Watchers estimated the figure of wasted spending on clothing to be £10 billion, or £200 per adult, with only 55 per cent of the clothes women own actually being worn. While some people may be hanging on to things for posterity, or 'just in case', there is undoubtedly a lot of hoarding of unworn or unnecessary clothing going on.

Before you begin organising your wardrobe, it is important to have a clear-out to eliminate old clothing that is no longer worn, so that you are only organising what you are going to wear. This process is crucial: it will free up space for the remaining clothes, enabling you to organise them better and find items easily. It will also help you to identify what gaps you may have in your wardrobe – garments that you may need to purchase to maximise the potential of what you currently have. Having a thorough wardrobe audit is also very liberating – it will make you feel much more organised and in control of your collection, your style and your life. The ends of seasons are the best times to have a clear-out, so you can do it at the same time as rotating your wardrobe and putting out-of-season clothes into storage.

Be realistic about the clothes that you wear day to day; hanging on to garments that you no longer wear takes up space unnecessarily, so try to adopt a ruthless sorting process. If you haven't worn an item in a year, ask yourself why you're holding on to these items; and if you don't have a good enough answer, get rid of them. Excess clothing will weigh you down spatially and mentally. It's fine to keep one or two old garments that have sentimental value, but don't let them dominate your wardrobe. If you have a lot of old vintage and valuable clothing that you are keeping for posterity, consider different long-term storage solutions – don't store them in your main wardrobe (see

Seasonal Storage section on page 109).

Go through your wardrobe and try on everything. Divide into piles:

1. Keep, wear regularly
2. Keep, but need to supplement with new purchases in order to wear
3. Wash/iron/mend
4. Sell
5. Charity
6. Storage
7. Discard/recycle

Group 2 is likely to be full of separates and, as explained earlier, separates only work if they have something to work with. Next time you go shopping, go with an idea of these wardrobe gaps that need to be filled, rather than being lured by the latest fashions or the sale rack with 70 per cent off.

If there are any items that are dirty or damaged or need altering, put these in group 3 and deal with them before returning them to the wardrobe or selling/donating to charity. If they need repairing or altering, you aren't going to wear them until they're fixed – nothing should be in the wardrobe that isn't ready to wear.

If garments no longer fit or you haven't worn them in a while, try selling them or donating to a charity shop. Selling unwanted clothing on eBay is a great way to find your unwanted garments a new home – after all, one lady's trash is another lady's treasure. Put eBay sales profits towards funding your new essential items for group 2. Popular designer and high-street labels and occasion outfits/dresses tend to sell better on eBay than casual clothes, so consider taking casual clothes straight to the charity shop – if they are in a good, wearable condition – or to a clothing recycling bank. High-end designer labels will also sell well on designer second-hand clothing websites (see Appendix I for web addresses). Worn-out clothing of an appropriate fabric, such as cotton, can be cut into rags to use for household cleaning or shoe polishing. Anything else should be recycled.

If you carry out a wardrobe audit in winter, make sure all your summer wear is placed in the storage pile, and vice versa (see Seasonal Storage on page 109 for tips on how to store clothing). Transitional items can be kept out for autumn/spring, when the weather is unpredictable.

Repeat the process for accessories – often accessories are bought without a thought for what to wear them with. Try to build up a collection of neutral accessories first, before purchasing coloured ones. If you have bags and shoes in black, tan/beige and white/cream, then you will always have matching accessories for any coloured outfit. It's worth investing more in shoes of these colours as you are likely to wear them more often than coloured shoes. The Queen has a large collection of brightly coloured clothing, but look at her footwear – rarely is she seen without her black patent heels in winter or white shoes in summer.

Many people have a cluttered underwear drawer because they hold on to items for years without wear, or they might have lots of odd socks hoping to be reunited with their lost other half. Go through your underwear drawer and throw away any old items that are not worn, such as bras that have lost their shape or no longer fit. Your underwear drawer should be ordered and tidied so that it is easy to locate what you need first thing in the morning. Try and have one drawer devoted purely

Recycling Clothes

Throwing away worn-out clothing is damaging to the environment – millions of garments end up in landfill each year. According to Oxfam, 9,513 garments are thrown into landfill in Britain every five minutes. That's a total of one billion items a year. As well as the environmental concern this causes (some textiles will emit harmful gases when they eventually biodegrade), there is a huge financial cost to landfill depositing: at £72 per tonne of landfill waste, the cost per year of throwing away clothing in the UK is over £25 million. Clothes and shoes can be recycled along with other household textiles and made into new textiles, such as household insulation or mattress filling. Some clothing will also be sold on for reuse in countries such as Africa. Check with your local council to see if they collect clothing for recycling, or look out for clothing recycle banks in supermarket car parks. Refer to the website www.recycle.com to find out what you can recycle and where. Some retailers, such as M&S (in partnership with Oxfam), Zara and H&M, run initiatives where you receive a store voucher in return for your unwanted clothing. TK Maxx also accept donations of unwanted clothes, which they pass on to Cancer Research UK to sell or recycle.

to underwear. As these items are small, you don't want them to get lost beneath larger garments or tangled with belts or other accessories. Drawer dividers can help to keep underwear organised, or if you only have shelves, then place items in an open shoebox or similar-sized container. See Appendix I for suggestions of underwear storage suppliers.

Cleaning the wardrobe space

To ensure that your clothes are kept in the best possible condition when not being worn, they need to be kept in the right environment, so it is important to thoroughly clean the inside of the wardrobe at least twice a year and dust it regularly. A build-up of dust will cause clothes to smell musty and will attract pests. When you rotate your clothing with the seasons, this is a good time to take out everything and give the wardrobe a deep clean. Use a vacuum cleaner inside and a damp cloth to remove dust and dirt. Leave open for a few hours to air thoroughly and do not put the clothes back in until the wardrobe is completely dry. Use hanging lavender sachets to maintain a fresh smell in the wardrobe and to deter moths. Clean drawer units in the same way and re-line with plain or lavender-scented lining paper. Once you have had a thorough trying-on and clearing-out session, and the wardrobe is clean and dry, you can begin reorganising your clothing within the wardrobe.

Organising clothes

For nothing matters except life; and,
of course, order.

THE COMMON READER, VIRGINIA WOOLF

Organisation and order are key to keeping a tidy and
accessible wardrobe. There are many different elements
you have to bring together to create an outfit, so the
process of dressing will be made a lot quicker and easier
if your wardrobe is kept in a tidy, orderly fashion at all
times. Once you have a system for organising and storing
your clothes, you will begin to value the things you have
and want to get the full potential out of each garment,
rather than resorting to buying something new when
you're looking for a new outfit to wear.

Hanging clothing

The best way to organise your clothing in your wardrobe
is to divide it into sections, such as workwear, casual
wear, evening wear and sportswear. Within these sections
organise garments by type (skirts/trousers/tops), and
then by colour, darks to lights. Keep separates grouped
together according to garment type to allow for mixing and
matching with other items as much as possible, but there
may be separates within evening wear or work/formal wear
that are clearly matching 'outfits', so these can be kept
together. Apart from these examples, I wouldn't advise
keeping outfits together as it limits your choices as to how
items can be worn, and will also spoil the streamlined
effect of arranging by garment type and colour.

Always align your hangers/clothes facing the same direction, with the hook facing the back of the wardrobe. Don't pack things in the wardrobe too tightly – clothes need space to air and hang freely to allow creases to fall out.

Evening dresses with very delicate fabrics and clothes that are only worn occasionally should be protected from dust with garment bags. Use breathable calico bags with a clear pocket on the front so that you can insert a photo or label detailing the garment. Or tie a luggage tag to the garment bag with details of the contents written on it. Do not store clothes in plastic clothing bags (such as those you get from the dry-cleaners) – the plastic will damage clothing fibres over time. Ensure that the garment bag is long enough for the garment, in order to prevent unnecessary creasing at the hem. Short plastic shoulder covers can be used to protect the tops of dresses, if you have lots of them and want to be able to view them all in your wardrobe. Very heavily beaded dresses should be laid in drawers rather than hung, as hanging them will cause the fabric to sag and stretch over time.

The following items should be hung in your wardrobe:

• Coats
• Jackets
• Suits
• Trousers
• Dresses
• Skirts
• Shirts (these can be folded, if you prefer)
• Dressy tops

Most skirts have little loops attached to the waistband so that they can be hung on shirt hangers. It is best to avoid this method, however, and to stick to clip hangers. Hanging skirts by these loops will distort the shape of the garment and create creasing around the waistband. It will also affect the alignment of the skirts in the wardrobe.

Trousers are best hung from the waist or hem using a clip hanger rather than a trouser hanger, which can cause creasing to the knee area. If you do use trouser hangers, place a sheet of tissue paper over the bar, to minimise creasing. The advantage of the trouser hanger is that the trousers will hang at a shorter level, so this might be more space efficient if you have a short hanging space. Whichever method you use, be consistent so that the trousers will align at the same level within the wardrobe.

Hangers
If you tend to keep the shop's hanger when buying new clothing it is likely that your wardrobe is full of hangers

of different sizes, shapes and colours. If you want your wardrobe to look neat and organised, it is best to discard all these hangers and use matching ones. This will keep the clothes hanging at an even level and make them look more streamlined on the rail.

Never use wire hangers (the type you get from dry-cleaners). Although they take up very little space in the wardrobe, the wire offers no support to the shoulder of the garment, so they will cause damage to this area of fabric, over time. Non-slip, slim, velour-covered plastic hangers, or slim rubber hangers, are my favourites due to their space efficiency. You'll be amazed at how much space you can free up in your wardrobe just by changing your hangers. See Appendix I for stockists. Choose a neutral colour and use the right hanger for the appropriate garment; heavy clothing, such as suit jackets and coats, will require a little more support in the shoulder area.

Different types of hangers

• **Shirt hanger** (also suitable for dresses and tops). Fasten at least every other button before hanging the shirt, to hold the shape of the garment.

• **Suit hanger with bar.** Used for jacket/trouser suits.

• **Suit with clip.** Used for skirt suits. Put acid-free tissue paper under the clips to protect delicate fabrics.

• **Trouser.** Hang with the seat/gusset pointing away from the front (for trousers with a crease, fold along the crease). Place a sheet of tissue paper over the bar of the hanger to prevent creasing.

• **Skirt/trouser.** Used for skirts and shorts. Can also be used for trousers. Again, use acid-free tissue paper under the clips to protect delicate fabrics. Make sure zips/buttons are done up to prevent the garment from stretching.

Folding clothing

Folding your clothing properly may seem tedious to begin with, but once you get used to it you will be able to do it much more quickly. It really is the key to a tidy and accessible wardrobe, so it's important to make the effort to get it right at an early stage.

The following items should be folded and placed on wardrobe shelves or in drawers:

• Knitwear, such as jumpers, cardigans
• T-shirts and casual tops
• Jeans
• Loungewear
• Sportswear
• Underwear

Open shelving units are better than deep drawers for displaying jumpers and T-shirts as you will be able to arrange these by type and colour and view each item more easily. Sort into groups, such as V-necks, crew-necks, roll-necks, T-shirts, cardigans and then into colour order: dark to light. Knitwear is always best kept folded to prevent the delicate fibres from stretching on a hanger.

Jeans are best kept folded on a shelf unit, either in thirds or quarters, depending on the quantity and size of the shelves.

Template-folding (box-folding)

The best way to fold knitwear, shirts, T-shirts and other casual tops is using a plastic folding template so that they are all folded to the same dimensions and look more ordered and organised once layered in a pile on a shelf

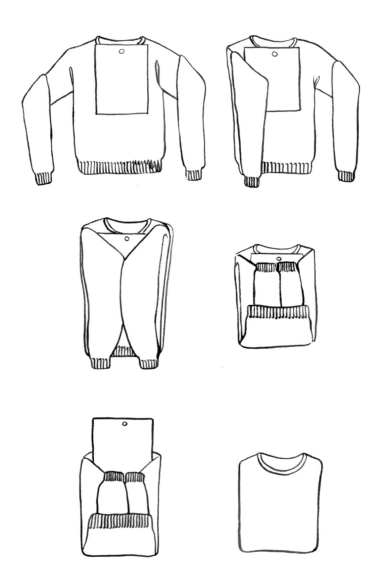

Template-folding

(see Appendix I for supplier list). Once you are more used to the folding technique, you can fold freehand without the aid of the template.

1. Place the item face down with the template centred on top and aligned with the neckline.
2. Fold the left side in, aligning with the edge of the template and fold the sleeve downwards.
3. Repeat for the right side, making sure the sleeves are aligned evenly and the cuffs are next to each other.
4. Fold the bottom half upwards so the cuffs meet the neckline.
5. Slide the template out. If the cuffs overlap at this point, then fold in so that the garment appears as a complete rectangle.
6. Turn it over and you are left with a perfectly folded garment.

If you are placing knitwear or T-shirts in a drawer, then you can roll up the box-folded sweater into thirds – this method utilises the space effectively when storing jumpers in drawers and has the advantage of there being no top or bottom to the pile, so each garment is easily visible and accessible. However, if you only have shelving space and no chest of drawers, then it is harder to organise the clothing this way. I prefer a tiered approach to arranging different tops so that you can see the neckline at a glance.

Lingerie folding
I have learned that it's the small things in life that matter, literally, including your smalls. If you're finding your wardrobe detox somewhat daunting, then start with your underwear drawer. I only have to spend ten minutes

organising my undies drawer to gain a feeling of control that motivates me to tackle the rest of my day's duties.

Lingerie doesn't require much folding, but if you take a small amount of time to arrange it neatly by type and colour, it will help when trying to locate specific items. Drawer organisers are useful for keeping different types of underwear separate, and preventing you from having a top drawer full of jumbled smalls.

Bras. Fold by pushing one cup inside the other with the straps tucked in behind. Ensure the cups of different bras are facing the same way when placed in the drawer. Place each bra slightly overlapping the one behind and arrange by colour. If they are padded, the shape will keep better if you arrange them in the drawer the way that they are worn.

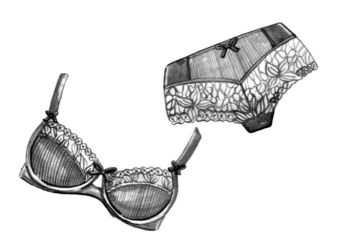

Knickers. Fold in half bottom to top and then fold the right side twice towards the centre. Tuck the bottom edge in diagonally, to achieve a neat line. Repeat with the other side until you have a neat rectangle. Arrange in a tiered fashion by type, e.g. shorts, bikini, and then by colour.

Folding socks

There are different ways of folding socks – choose whichever method suits you and your space. Box-folding takes a bit of practice to perfect but it is the tidiest way of folding thicker, longer socks (like welly socks or shooting socks), and also helps with the process of putting on long socks, as your foot goes straight into the foot area of the sock. It has the advantage of keeping the socks flat, ready to wear and easy to pack when travelling. The socks are folded individually, so it might not be the best method if you are prone to losing odd socks.

To box-fold socks:

1. Put the sock over your right hand completely, like a puppet.
2. Pinch the top of the sock with your left hand and lower your right hand out of the sock until you get to the heel. Now pinch the heel with your right hand (still in the sock) and with your left hand, pull the rest of the sock from the hem inside out.
3. Straighten up by inserting your hand into the inside-out sock.
4. Repeat with the other sock and place one on top of the other.
5. The sock will now be inside out, so when you place your foot in, you can pull it on with ease.
   (For photos illustrating this process refer to www.theladysmaid.com.)

With long socks you will have to fold back half of the sock after step 3, to achieve a smaller neat rectangle. **Alternatively:** Fold together by putting one sock on top of the other. Fold in half by bringing the tip of the toe up to the cuff, then take the cuff of one sock and turn the remaining folds inside out. The sock will not be as flat and straight as the box-folding method, so thick socks will appear bulky when folded like this, but this method has the advantage of keeping the socks together in a pair.

Foot-socks/sports socks

Pair up with the opening at the top and fold the top one into thirds inside the bottom one, to make a neat semi-circle shape.

Tights

Fold in half side to side, then in half and quarters, foot to waistband. Once in quarters, roll fold until you have a neat rectangle. Arrange by denier and then by colour – light to dark.

Tight footsies

As for foot-socks, but fold the sides inwards to get a neat semi-circle.

Swimwear

Fold bikinis as you would underwear – to keep matching tops and bottoms together, consider storing in individual bikini bags, especially when travelling. Swimming costumes can be box-folded as you would a vest.

*I sat down on the bed, my little suitcase with
all my worldly possessions neatly folded inside,
looked around at all the empty splendour of my
new surroundings ... and burst into tears.*

HILDA NEWMAN, LADY'S MAID TO THE COUNTESS
OF COVENTRY AT CROOME COURT, 1935–39

Hilda Newman spent four years in the service of Nesta
Donne, Countess of Coventry and wife of the 10th Earl,
George Coventry, at the family's eighteenth-century grand
Palladian mansion house, Croome Court in Worcestershire.
Like Rose Harrison, Hilda had humble roots before she was
immersed in this grand setting. Growing up in the town
of Stamford in Lincolnshire, she remembers her mother
washing clothes in the kitchen sink – scrubbing them
clean by hand. Her grandfather was a professional tailor,
so from an early age Hilda was exposed to the process of
making and caring for clothes. On leaving school, Hilda
was apprenticed to a local dressmaker at the age of 15,
learning the trade from the bottom by picking up pins off
the floor and removing tacks from clothes. After this four-
year apprenticeship, Hilda worked briefly and unhappily
in a local hotel laundry before a colleague suggested her
dressmaking skills might be better suited to the role of a
lady's maid. Hilda replied to an advertisement that her
colleague showed her and was subsequently offered the job
as lady's maid to the Countess of Coventry.

As a senior servant, Hilda didn't take meals with the
junior staff in the servants' hall; meals were served to
her by a kitchen maid in a separate room (the Steward's
Room), where she would eat amongst the rest of the senior

staff – the children's governess, the butler and the cook/
housekeeper. Hilda even had a maid to wake her up in
the morning at 7 a.m., bring her tea and run her bath – a
luxury not only because it was run for her, but because at
her family home, she was used to 'a quick dip in the old tin
tub' in front of the fire once a week. Hilda became aware
of the household hierarchy – not just between 'upstairs
and downstairs', but perhaps more importantly within the
staff below stairs – each member knowing their place and
respecting those above and below them in rank.

Hilda had a large bedroom where she set up an ironing
board to press the countess's clothes, a task made easier
with the invention of the electric iron. Although widely used
in more affluent houses, Hilda's prior experience of pressing
had been with the more cumbersome cast iron at home in
Lincolnshire. Among the usual wardrobe duties of preparing
and laying out clothes, the countess also required Hilda to
brush her hair for one hour every morning and half an hour
before dinner, a task she found 'tiresome and distinctly
boring'. Laying out clothes also meant laying out underwear,
and while the average number of undergarments for a lady
had decreased by the beginning of the twentieth century, by
1935 they were still numerous items in comparison to the
present day – Hilda would lay out five undergarments for the
countess: knickers, a girdle, stockings, a slip and a petticoat.
A day or evening dress would also be laid out, alongside
accessories to match, including a bag, jewellery, gloves, a
hat and perhaps a fan in summer or a fur in winter. So there
could be as many as a dozen items for each outfit change.

During Hilda's initial days and weeks at Croome, she was
struck with homesickness, and referred to her new home
and place of work as 'a prison'. She soon settled into life
in service, however, and expressed a sadness at having to
leave Croome Court when she and her mistress signed up

Hilda Newman, Lady's Maid to the Countess of Coventry, in 1937.

to the Auxiliary Territorial Service in 1939, to do their bit for the war effort: 'I was going to lose my home and, with it, everything I had loved. Because I had grown to love the place. I treasured the times when I was free to wander over the vast estate – a place of wonder and peace and tranquility.'

A role in service such as Hilda's not only provided steady employment, it also provided a home and friendship amongst fellow staff. In Hilda's case, she also met her husband, Roland, chauffeur to the Coventrys. After four years, Hilda had witnessed how a role in service had become all-encompassing – a way of life and not just a job.

With the outbreak of the Second World War, the lavish lifestyles of the English aristocracy were entering their dying days. Post-war austerity and rising house maintenance bills saw more grand estates like Croome being sold and their owners streamlining their staff. The lady's maid – once an essential attendant to every great lady in the land – was all but dispensed with.

Organising accessories

I did NOT have three thousand pairs of shoes,
I had one thousand and sixty.

IMELDA MARCOS

Shoes and boots

Shoes often form an extensive part of many ladies'
wardrobes; the average woman in Britain owns 20 pairs
of shoes, with some ladies devoting entire wardrobes
and rooms exclusively to their storage and display. You
may not need an entire room to display your shoes, but
it is important to store them properly so that they aren't
exposed to unnecessary damage from dust. Shoeboxes are
the best way to protect them, but this is impractical for
every pair as you will want them to be easily accessible
within your wardrobe. The best place to store everyday
shoes so that you can see and access them easily is at the
bottom of your wardrobe or on shelving units or racks.

If you have a lot of space to display shoes then try to
arrange them into style groups (flats, court shoes, sandals,
wedges, ankle boots etc.) and then arrange by colour
within these groups. If your shoe collection is very big and
you don't have room to display all of them easily, store
the dressier pairs in boxes. You could even take a photo of
them and fix to the front of the shoebox so that you don't
have to search through lots of boxes to find the pair you're
looking for. Front-opening transparent boxes are good so
that you can easily access each box when stacked in a
pile. If storing shoes in boxes, remember to line the shoe
with rolled-up tissue paper, or a shoe-shaper, which will
hold the shape of the shoe. When packing shoes for travel,
always place inside a shoe dust bag (most designer shoes

are sold with a shoe bag, or you could buy them separately or make your own). The shoe bag serves to protect both the shoe and the surrounding garments within your suitcase. See Appendix I for shoe storage ideas.

Handbags

Handbags, like shoes, form an extensive part of many ladies' wardrobes. Clever display will ensure that even the smallest clutch bag is not lost in the deep recesses of the wardrobe. Unlike shoes, handbags come in so many different shapes and sizes that it can sometimes be challenging to display them to best effect. Bags will also often be sold with a dust bag to protect them – make sure you keep hold of all these bags in a safe place as they are handy when packing for travel.

Shelving units within the wardrobe are the best place to store handbags – make sure you have some units that are 'tall' enough to store larger bags. Arrange as you would clothing: a section for evening bags, one for day bags, and arrange by colour within each section. Bags often come with padding or tissue paper inside to support their shape. It is a good idea to keep these inside larger bags, to maintain their shape. Boot and bag shapers can be bought to serve the same purpose. If you use multiple bags, try to get into the habit of emptying them when you return home, to prevent clutter building up inside and to allow for easy transfer of essential items, such as wallet and phone. Some handbag retailers, such as Hermès, even sell a transferable inner pouch lining to make this process easier.

Belts, scarves and gloves

Accessories like belts and scarves complement and complete an outfit, so a 'look' can appear completely new or updated just by changing your accessories. They can be awkward to store properly, especially if you have many of them, but try and find a way that suits your space to keep them as ordered as possible so that when it comes to accessorising your outfit, you can easily find what you're looking for.

Belts are best stored in a shallow drawer rolled up and arranged by colour. You could place each belt in a drawer organiser, as with underwear. If you don't have space in drawers, you could hang them on special belt hangers within the wardrobe, or in a storage box on a wardrobe shelf.

Scarves can be folded and arranged in drawers or stacked on shelves, arranged by colour, as with knitwear. Display gloves in a shallow drawer: arrange by colour and group different fabrics together.

Costume jewellery

Costume jewellery is a fun and cheap way of your accessorising outfits. It differs from fine jewellery as it is generally made of cheaper metals and plastics, rather than gold, silver and precious jewel stones (see pp. 165–6 for tips on the storage and cleaning of fine jewellery).

Costume jewellery should still be stored properly as the metals are less durable than fine jewellery, so need to be protected if they are to last.

Necklaces can be placed within jewellery divider trays in drawers – trays with different-sized compartments are good, to prevent different items getting tangled. Acrylic jewellery chests and stackable trays are another good option; the transparent plastic makes it easy to view the contents. (See Appendix I for suggested suppliers.)

It is advisable to put jewellery away after wear rather than displaying it on exposed jewellery trees or stands as these will just attract dust.

Hats

Occasion hats will usually be sold in a hatbox. Keep them stored in these as this is the best way to protect them. Fill the crown with tissue paper, to keep its shape, and fill the space around the hat with tissue paper to protect it. Other everyday hats, such as wool beanies or flat caps, can be placed on high shelves within the wardrobe.

Wardrobe inventory

One of the duties of a lady's maid is to keep an inventory of all the clothing and accessories that belong to her employer. This is important because the quantity of clothing that some ladies keep is very great, and can be spread over several different homes, so unless a central record is kept it can be difficult to quickly trace specific outfits. Outfit log books are also sometimes kept to record outfits worn for different occasions, thus preventing the lady from wearing the same outfit to the same event twice. You may not feel this is necessary for your wardrobe, but if you do have a very large wardrobe collection, creating an inventory will help you to keep track of its contents. Recording clothing details is also useful if you decide to sell an item at a later date, or for insurance purposes. If you have many expensive designer dresses, shoes and bags, it is worth keeping the original receipts alongside your inventory to make valuation easier. Start by taking photos of each item, including accessories. Note down as many details as possible about each one, e.g. designer, fabric, price, date bought. Keep a computerised inventory with a file for each garment type; you may also want to print it out in book form, or keep in a file with the photographs attached. You could also import your photographic catalogue into an easy-to-view online wardrobe using special computer software, such as HomyFads Wardrobe Manager (for Windows) or Stylebook (for iPhone/iPad). These apps also enable you to style outfits from your virtual wardrobe and plan packing for trips.

Keeping organised

To keep your clothing collection organised in the future, try to resist purchasing any unnecessary items and focus instead on filling the gaps in your wardrobe that were revealed after the clear-out. Make a list of things you think your existing wardrobe would benefit from and focus on acquiring these items the next time you go shopping. Your goal is for a complete, versatile and manageable wardrobe to fit in with your space and lifestyle. Resist the temptation to purchase new, one-off garments, unless you think they will complement what you already own. See The Lady's Maid's Capsule Wardrobe (on pages 32–42) for ideas on how to build a wearable clothing collection.

Another way of keeping control over your new tidy wardrobe is to always get rid of something every time you buy something new. Unless you have unlimited space, this is the only way that you will keep the size of your collection at a constant and prevent overcrowding. By selling the old item on eBay, this will also make you feel more justified in making a new purchase, as you have given yourself a discount tag!

Try to appreciate the items that you do have – this doesn't mean that you have to wear the same thing over and over again. Rather, if you have a well-organised and versatile wardrobe, you should be able to wear one garment in many different ways – dressing it up or down, or wearing it with different accessories. In this way, you will create many different 'outfits' without having to buy new clothes.

As with cleaning, if you do it little and often, clothing organisation won't become such a chore. Make sure you put away worn clothing daily and don't let it pile up in heaps. It is a good idea to leave an outfit out overnight to let it air, but if it doesn't need washing, then put it back in the wardrobe the next day. Also, fold and put away laundry as soon as it is done.

Long-term storage – wedding dresses

For long-term storage of precious garments, such as wedding dresses or christening gowns, fold the fabric using acid-free tissue paper and store in acid-free storage boxes. Do not use ordinary cardboard boxes as these may contain harmful chemicals that will cause yellowing over time. As the garment will be stored for a long period without wear, it is at risk of permanent creasing, so don't hold back with the tissue paper – fill the arms and bodice with rolled-up sheets and fold the veil and train with layers of tissue paper to protect it as much as possible. It is advisable to check on the dress every year or so to inspect for any damage – this is also an opportunity to re-fold the garment along slightly different lines to minimise the risk of permanent creasing. If you are storing a very valuable vintage garment for a long time that has metal buttons, wrap each individual button with tissue paper to prevent them from staining the fabric.

Seasonal storage

One of the ways to maximise the space available in your wardrobe, and make it easier to find clothing that is wearable according to the current climate, is to rotate your clothes with the season – pack away winter clothes as summer approaches, and vice versa. If only wearable clothes are visible, it will help you to locate outfits more quickly. If you don't have extra wardrobe space for out-of-season clothing, you can fold the clothes and place in storage bags or boxes. Use bags or boxes specifically manufactured for storing clothes as these will best protect them. You can find these in department stores or household storage companies online (see Appendix I).

Clothes are vulnerable to damage when in storage if they are not protected properly, so it is important to take the correct steps to prepare them.

• Ensure everything going into storage is washed, clean and thoroughly dry. Any clothes with food stains or traces of perspiration, or damp, will attract moths and other bugs.

• Never store clothes in polythene or plastic bags – condensation will eventually form, causing mould or discolouration damage to the fabric. Storage bags should be made of breathable fabric, such as calico.

• If storing clothes in boxes or suitcases, fold and wrap clothing with acid-free, white tissue paper, to provide protection and prevent too much long-term creasing.

• Extra care should be paid to moth-prone fabrics, such as wool and cashmere – store these separately to other clothing, preferably in knitwear storage bags (see Appendix I for stockists) and place an anti-moth lavender sachet in each storage bag or box (see Caring for Cashmere on page 150).

• Keep all storage containers in a cool, damp-free area, away from sunlight and heat: above wardrobes or under beds are the most obvious places. Don't store in attics as it is hard to control their environmental conditions.

• If you are likely to be visiting warmer climes during the winter months it is a good idea to keep holiday clothes together in one storage box so that they will be easy to locate when the time comes to pack.

Pack like a pro

I am a seasoned pro when it comes to packing – I have been known to pack ten suitcases in the time it takes for my boss to have breakfast, whilst also being afflicted with jet lag and recovering from the after-effects of a mild electric shock in Bangkok. But if the thought of packing sends you into a cold sweat, worry not: follow the practical advice below to ease pre-travel stress and ensure that your clothes are kept in tip-top condition in transit and on arrival at your destination.

Top tips for stress-free packing

• Don't over-pack. You might be going on holiday, away for the weekend, or on a business trip – you're not moving home, so be selective when packing clothing for trips. Think about what you're going to be doing on the trip and what the weather will be like, and pack accordingly. Plan outfits in advance – bring a selection of clothing out of your wardrobe and think about what will work together for the trip. Separates that can be mixed and matched are a good idea in order to maximise outfit opportunities. (See Styling a Summer Holiday Wardrobe on page 45.)

• If you are packing delicate, beaded or crease-prone garments, use acid-free tissue paper to protect the fabric and minimise the risk of creasing. Pack heavier items at the bottom of the case (shoes, bags) and lighter clothing items at the top.

• Try to fold garments along natural seam lines as much as possible, to minimise creasing. Avoid vertical folds, as these do not fall out as naturally.

• Pack trousers by folding the trouser leg half in the case and half out, and then continue to pack clothing. Once the case is full, fold the outer part of the trouser in. This will prevent you from having to fold the trouser leg on itself, which would create a crease.

• Lingerie/laundry bags are a good way of keeping underwear together in the suitcase for ease of packing/ unpacking.

• Dust bags for shoes and handbags are also worth using, to protect the contents and the surrounding clothes.

If you travel regularly, it is well worth keeping a travel toiletry bag separate from your main home toiletries so that you don't have the extra bother of having to constantly pack these items every time you travel.

Pack large bottled liquids in zip-lock bags before placing in toiletry bags for added security – if there is any leakage your clothing will be protected. I once lost an entire (loosely stoppered) new bottle of perfume to the contents of my suitcase ... On the plus side, everything smelt nice on arrival!

Hanging toiletry bags with transparent pockets for make-up are also great for travel, as you can hang them straight up and easily locate their contents (Marks & Spencer sell good value ones).

Before leaving for the airport, check the weight of your bag with a hand-held weighing scale – find out your airline's weight limits for baggage to ensure that you won't be lumbered with an excess baggage fee.

Lighten the load – travel toiletries and make-up

Travelling light is not easy even for the most seasoned travellers and it is expensive to be caught out at the airport with an extra charge for a heavy suitcase. One area where you can lighten the load is with your travel toiletries and make-up, so take note of these top tips for toiletry packing:

• Pack miniatures of your essential daily toiletries and full-sized bottles only of those you'll use more of, such as sun protection.
• Many brands do ready-made travel sets complete with zipped transparent bags, which are great as they are permitted in hand luggage. Only buy these if you're actually going to use all the products or remove those you won't use on holiday and leave them at home.
• If you are loyal to a particular brand and can't do without it, decant small amounts into empty miniature pumpable, squeezable and sprayable bottles. Most chemists and some department stores sell these.
• Streamline your skincare routine. Pack only the products you actually use on a daily basis. Most hotels will have a decent shower gel, so you could dispense with your usual brands for a short period in order to save space.
• Pack your toiletries in a transparent bag so that you can easily see what you have and whether any items are missing.
• Be selective. In a hot climate you are unlikely to wear your usual make-up, especially in the daytime when your skin is exposed to the sun. Try and stick to just a few of your most worn items, such as tinted moisturiser, mascara, lipstick/tint and blusher and/or bronzer.

PART III
CARE OF
CLOTHING AND
ACCESSORIES

Clothing care

Clothing care needn't be seen as a chore. If you have chosen your garments well and own things that you love and value, then you should want to treat them with care and attention in order to preserve their lives and continue to benefit from wearing them, as well as to respect the money you originally spent on them. A little knowledge in the skills of washing, ironing and mending will ensure that everything in your wardrobe is fit to wear for many years.

Clothing is made from textiles produced from a variety of different fibres – natural, synthetic or a combination of both. The type of fibre dictates how different items of clothing should be washed and treated, to ensure the optimum lifespan of a garment. Regular washing is necessary as it will improve not only the appearance and smell of garments, it will help prevent damage from pests such as moths that are particularly attracted to dirty clothing.

A balance should be struck, however, as excessive washing, particularly in a machine, is likely to wear the garment out sooner. If garments appear clean and smell fresh, then it is only necessary to brush them down with a clothing brush to eliminate tiny dust and dirt particles. Brushing will also revive the nap of clothing such as wool suits. Fabric refresher sprays are an option to reduce the frequency of washing clothing, as their odour neutralisers help to keep textiles smelling freshly laundered. You could spray clothing with lavender linen spray for a more natural alternative, with the added benefit of deterring moths.

Top tips for daily clothing care

• After clothes have been worn, inspect them for any visible stains or damage. Check the hems and buttons especially. If clothes need mending, see to it ASAP, before putting away/washing.

• If clothes are stained, treat the stain according to its type (see Stain Removal on page 133) and then wash, if necessary.

• If clothes don't need washing or mending, brush them down to get rid of any loose hairs and dust. Lint rollers are good for removing hairs, or use a stiff clothes brush for suits and coats.

• If possible, leave worn clothes hanging out overnight to air – even if the clothes aren't visibly dirty, they will have traces of perspiration and other odours that could attract bugs.

• Remember to always empty pockets before putting away/washing. If clothes are clean, fasten buttons and zips to hold the shape of the garment, fold and put away.

LADIES' MAIDS AND THE NATIONAL TRUST

ELLENOR (NELLIE) ROGERS AND HARRIET ROGERS,
LADIES' MAIDS AT ERDDIG HOUSE

In 1881 Ellenor Rogers became junior lady's maid to Etheldred and Agneta, the daughters of Simon and Victoria Yorke at Erddig House in Wales. In 1888, Ellenor moved on to work for a family in Ayrshire before joining a wealthy American family with whom she travelled the world. She even had the chance to a camel with her employers in Egypt. Ellenor kept stationery from all of the luxury hotels in which she stayed as souvenirs of her visits – places she visited included the Waldorf Astoria in New York; The Grand Hotel, Cairo; and The Metropole Hotel, Monaco. Like Rose Harrison at Cliveden (see p. 72), Ellenor's servant role was unique in that it gave her – a humble Welsh girl – the opportunity to travel the world and broaden her horizons beyond the confines of the servants' hall.

As the daughter of an Erddig carpenter, Harriet was born on the Erddig estate and gave the Yorke family 44 years of service from 1852–96. Initially serving as a nursemaid, she was promoted to Victoria Yorke's lady's maid in 1859. Like her niece, Harriet also travelled around Europe with the Yorkes. After many years of service as a lady's maid, she changed roles again within the household to that of cook/ housekeeper. In retirement, Harriet assisted Philip Yorke II with compiling his servant poems of 1911 and 1912, one of which was written about her:

> … *Then, greatly by the Mistress praised,*
> *She to an upper place was raised,*

And thus for twelve more years she stayed
Filling the post of Ladies' Maid:
Then a vocation she did find
As Cook and Housekeeper combined;
Which lasted nigh for years a score,
Till her last Patrons were no more …

Harriet Rogers (left) and Ellenor Rogers (right) pictured in the servant staff photo in the garden of Erddig House, 1887.

Washing

Rainwater was collected in two huge wooden barrels from off the roof. It was carried by bucket to the copper, a brick-built boiler in a corner of the wash-house and heated by a coke fire from a grate underneath. When it was boiling hot the water was transferred to a long wooden tub where clothes were carefully washed by hand ... when clean, the clothes were transformed into three different tubs for rinsing ... then they were put through the mangle and hung on two large angled clothes-lines in the garden where they were dried in the cleanest of country air.

THE LADY'S MAID: MY LIFE IN SERVICE, ROSINA HARRISON

If doing the laundry is not your favourite chore of the week, spare a thought for Rosina Harrison's mother's generation, whose task was much more arduous than ours is today. Rosina Harrison was Lady Astor's lady's maid at Cliveden from 1929–64 (see page 72), but in the quote above she is recalling the laundry workload of her mother. Monday was traditionally laundry day in many households, and without the aid of hot running water or the modern washing machine, which wasn't in use in the majority of households until the 1940s and 1950s, everything would be washed by hand – a physically demanding job that resulted in chapped and scalded hands. Thankfully, with the advances of technology, the domestic laundry load has been lightened and hand-washing is only now necessary for the most delicate of garments.

When washing clothes, it is important to match a
suitable washing procedure with the fabric type/level of
dirt. Strong fibres, such as cotton, can withstand higher
temperatures, and can be spun dry, tumble-dried and
ironed on a high setting. Delicate fibres, such as silk,
however, are vulnerable when wet and should be treated
carefully by washing at lower temperatures – without
wringing – and ironed with a cool iron.

Clothing care labels

Always follow the care instructions found on the label of
the garment. Even if you are experienced with clothing
care and can recognise fabrics instantly, it is always best
to double check. The label will tell you what the garment
is made of and how it should be washed, dried and ironed.
Refer to the chart in Appendix II to recognise different
care symbols and their meanings.

Preparing clothes for washing

• Check pockets are empty
• Close buttons and zips
• Brush off surplus dirt or dust
• If you notice damage, repair before washing
• Turn garments inside out

Types of detergent

There are three product types used for washing clothing:
powder, liquid or tabs. Choose according to preference,
as there are pros and cons to each. It is a good idea to
stock a variety of different detergents for all of your
laundry needs.

If you have a large household where washing is a regular occurrence, washing powder may be the most economical choice for most everyday washing. Be sure to keep an eye on the washing-machine drawer and clean it regularly, as powder can build up and be hard to remove if not dealt with.

Liquid detergents are good for pre-treating stains and are less likely to leave streaks that are sometimes caused by powder residue. Mild liquid detergents should always be used for delicate fabrics, as washing powders contain ingredients that could be harmful to their delicate fibres.

Tabs are handy because they contain a pre-measured amount of detergent, but they are the most expensive option.

• Pre-wash detergent, e.g. Vanish, is used to aid protein-based and other organic stain removal. It is effective at higher temperatures, so isn't suitable for delicate fabrics. Stained garments should be soaked in the pre-wash detergent/water solution for at least half an hour, before rinsing and washing as normal. Ensure the water is a cool temperature for protein-based stains as hot water will set stains.

• Biological detergent contains enzymes which increase the cleaning power. This is the best choice for stain removal, so is good for sports kits and heavily stained garments. The enzymes break down amino acids in protein-based stains such as food. Bio detergents shouldn't be used on delicate fabrics. Some people find that bio detergents irritate their skin – if this is the case, switch to non-bio.

• Non-biological detergent does not contain enzymes, so it is less effective at stain removal. It is, however, less likely to irritate those with sensitive skin.

• Delicates detergent is a liquid detergent for use with delicate fibres, such as wool and silk.

• Fabric conditioner reduces static and increases softness. Avoid using when washing towels as it decreases their absorbency. Check the machine drawer and clean it regularly to prevent build-up. White vinegar has fabric-softening properties and can be used as a natural alternative.

Water temperature

Always ensure that the correct water temperature is selected for the fabric type – refer to the care label. Most fabrics can be washed at 30 or 40 degrees. Where possible, wash at low temperatures, as this is more environmentally friendly and economical. Heavily-stained fabrics, however, will require washing at a higher heat. As a rule, the more delicate the fabric is, the less it is able to withstand heat, so silks and wools should always be washed at lower temperatures. Cottons and linens are made of stronger fibres, which can withstand higher temperatures.

Machine washing

Washing machines can sometimes appear a little overwhelming, with so many dials and options. Each machine is different, so always read the manufacturer's manual. The wash dial usually has different settings for washing different types of fabrics – these settings are programmed to adjust the water temperature and the length of the wash and spin, according to what different fabrics can withstand. The spin can usually also be adjusted manually, as can the temperature, if you prefer to wash things at a lower temperature with a slow spin. I wash all my clothes on the slowest spin speed.

Always divide clothing into three groups before washing: darks, colours, lights/whites, and into groups with the same wash symbol, where possible. If you are washing a mix of fabric types, choose the washing procedure for the most delicate fabric. Mixed-colour loads are possible if you include a 'colour catcher', which will absorb any run of dye from coloured clothing and prevent transfer to lighter coloured garments (see Appendix I for details). These are handy and time-saving, but it's still advisable to wash new, brightly coloured garments with similar colours as the colour will be more intense when new, so any loss of dye will be more noticeable. If you are using a powder or liquid detergent, do not overdose the washing machine with detergent as this will result in an excess of soap residue that could damage both the clothing and the machine. Follow the manufacturer's dosing guide and use the right amount of washing powder according to the weight of your washing load and how dirty it is. Do not overload the washing machine with clothing as this will affect the washing efficiency. Always treat any stains before

Top tip
To maintain your washing machine, run the machine empty every now and then on its hottest wash with a cup of white vinegar. White vinegar is an excellent natural cleaning agent and will help prevent bacteria and limescale building up within the machine.

loading into the machine and use fabric conditioner if desired, to add softness to the fabric and minimise static. If colour does run into a garment, then re-wash the item immediately before the dye sets.

Hand-washing – delicates

All delicate fabrics, such as cashmere, silk, lace and delicate underwear, should ideally be hand-washed in cool water. The fibres of these fabrics are most at risk from damage if exposed to excess heat and agitation from washing machines. If there is a hand-wash/delicates setting on your machine, you can use this for certain garments (refer to the care label). Make sure the spin cycle is minimised to the lowest setting – the whole wash should be slow and short to prevent agitating the fabric too much. Placing wool or silk garments in a large mesh bag within the wash will offer further protection from friction within the machine. Mesh bags are also advisable for any garments that have delicate trims, and for bras and tights, to prevent them getting tangled up with other garments inside the machine. Aside from silk and wool, there are some synthetic/semi-synthetic fibres that should be treated as 'delicates': viscose, rayon and acetate. These textiles are fragile and should be treated as you would silk or wool. Modal, Spandex and Lycra should also be treated as delicates.

If you prefer to wash by hand, always use a specially formulated, gentle liquid detergent suitable for hand-washing and make sure that the detergent is dissolved thoroughly in the water before adding the clothing (add hot water first to dissolve the detergent, and then top up with cold water to achieve a cool temperature). Do not rub delicate fabrics – silk fibres especially will weaken when wet, so are at risk of damage. Wool garments can also become distorted if not handled carefully when wet. Turn the garment inside out and gently squeeze the garment through the water/detergent. Rinse in cool water to remove all traces of the detergent. Do not wring dry, as this will cause structural damage to the fibres. Instead, roll gently in a drying towel, or dab with a towel to remove excess moisture, and then leave to dry naturally on a dry towel. Remember to re-shape the garment while still damp.

Drying clothes

Where possible, hang clothes to dry naturally – avoid using tumble-driers for clothing as these can shrink or damage items. Heated drying stands are great for drying clothes in winter. When machine washing clothing, even if it isn't delicate, I advise adjusting the spin settings on the washing machine to a lower setting so that clothes aren't damaged by a harsh spin – sometimes the hems on garments such as cotton T-shirts can become stretched and distorted if spun too much. To minimise creasing and regain the original shape and size, hang garments upside down – e.g. trousers by the ankles and shirts by the waistband. Some creases will then fall out naturally during the drying process, which reduces the amount of work that the iron will have to do. Delicate fabrics should be re-shaped while damp and left to dry naturally on a towel. Do not hang silks or woollens, as the fabric will stretch while wet – lay these garments flat on a towel to dry.

Some fabrics (such as wool suits and coats, or delicate beaded silks) are not washable and should be dry-cleaned only. Check the garment care label. Use a reputable company, as you want the garment to be treated in the best possible way. As the name indicates, the process of dry-cleaning involves cleaning clothes without adding water; it is not a completely 'dry' process, however, as dirt is removed using a cleaning fluid solvent. The solvents used are strong, so dry-cleaning will be damaging to textile fibres if done too often. Try to use as only a last resort for very delicate items, if you are unable to remove stains yourself (see Stain Removal section on page 133), or for suits/coats/dresses at the end of each season, prior to putting into storage.

Ironing

Ironing can be a therapeutic exercise for some people, when done in moderation. Satisfaction can be gained from seeing a crinkled item transform into a perfectly smooth, ironed and folded garment. But for many people, it is the nemesis of clothing care – especially ironing shirts. For ironing-board novices, it can be difficult to know where to begin, and it can seem that the more you iron, the more creases appear. Try to see it as a meditative, mindful process rather than a repetitive one – it is the final stage in the clothing care cycle towards bringing your garment back to its former glory, so don't give up yet!

After a garment has been washed and dried it will usually need to be ironed before returning to the wardrobe. Cottons and linens, in particular, will require ironing as these textiles crease the most during the washing process. Ironing is a straightforward process and garments will not be damaged, provided you always check that the heat level from the iron is appropriate for the fabric type. Excessive heat from an iron can ruin delicate fabrics within seconds, so always check the garment label and the heat of the iron before proceeding. Remember: the garment label is there for a reason – if it says a low heat is required, then follow this advice – don't think that the job will be done quicker with a hotter iron. Some fibres won't just be weakened from a hot iron, they will literally melt before your eyes.

Preparation for ironing

Fill the water vestibule of the iron with water. If you are in a hard water area, distilled water is recommended to prevent mineral deposits building up in the iron. Ensure the base of the iron is clean – any marks will transfer to the fabric and could stain it. Ensure you have a well-

Top tip

For those Iron Ladies who are not for turning, consider buying shirts with some synthetic content, e.g. polycotton, which are not as prone to creasing as 100 per cent cotton, and therefore much easier to iron. You can also straighten stubborn collars with hair-straighteners, to avoid getting the iron and ironing board out – be careful only to do this on strong fabric such as cotton.

covered ironing board; if it isn't padded enough, the metal structure could imprint onto the garment being ironed. Silver covers retain heat from the iron, effectively ironing both sides at once. If ironing more than one garment, start with the item that needs the coolest setting first, so that you don't have to wait for a higher setting to cool off each time. After consulting the care label in order to select the appropriate heat setting, test the iron on a small section of the garment, if ironing it for the first time.

Ironing technique

Damp clothes iron more easily, so try to keep clothing in a damp state. If your garment begins to dry, use a spray bottle filled with water to add moisture. Iron any lining first and then the reverse side of the fabric. Iron the 'right' side last, to minimise the risk of creases forming during the ironing process. Some delicate fabrics, such as silk and wool, should only be ironed on the reverse side, to prevent causing shiny marks. The care label will tell you if this is the case. Avoid pressing too hard around seams and pockets when ironing on the reverse, in order to minimise causing seam imprints on the right side of the garment. Alternatively, use a cotton pressing cloth to protect the top side of the garment when ironing. Pressing cloths will also protect the surface of delicate fabrics from heat damage from a hot iron. Some fabrics such as rayon cannot be ironed on the reverse as they will stick to the iron – once again, check the care label.

Iron using continuous movements – do not allow the iron to become stationary as you risk burning the fabric. Once ironed, leave clothes hanging to air for a while, as steam from the iron will have made the clothes a little damp.

Maintaining your iron

Empty the water container after use to prevent limescale from forming. Clean the iron regularly so the metal plate doesn't get sticky – use a special iron cleaning product, such as Hot Iron Cleaner (available from Lakeland).

How to iron a shirt in five minutes

I have devised a five-step technique to remove the stress as well as the creases from the ironing process. Before you start, remember these points:
• It is always best to iron a shirt when it is still slightly damp after washing. If it has dried, give it a quick spray all over with water from a spray bottle to dampen it (you can purchase these in chemists or supermarkets).
• Cotton can withstand high settings on the iron, so turn it up to the cotton setting, and if you have a steam iron, put the steam on. If you iron shirts a lot then it's really worth investing in a good steam iron as they are much more effective on stubborn creases.
With the ironing five-step order listed below, the smaller areas are dealt with first before moving on to the larger areas. This way it won't matter if any creases are formed in the bulk of the shirt during the ironing process, as they will be eliminated last.

1. **Collar.** Iron the underside first, then the outside.
2. **Yoke.** This is the area between the shoulders, at the top of the back. Place the shirt over the narrow part of the board and press the iron from one shoulder towards the back, then repeat on the other side.
3. **Cuffs.** Open buttons and iron inside and then outside.

4. **Sleeves.** Iron the cuff opening side first and then the reverse.
5. **Body.** Iron the front panels first using the tip of the iron to press around the buttons, then iron the back section. Use the widest part of the ironing board, so that you cover as much fabric as possible with just a few sweeps of the iron.

Steaming

Upright steamers are excellent for eliminating creases quickly from suits and dresses, especially long evening dresses that are harder to iron on a board. Steamers are particularly good for de-creasing awkward areas that are hard to reach with the iron without re-creasing the rest of the garment. If you have a lot of silk dresses or blouses, it is worth investing in a portable steamer as it is much quicker than ironing. Steaming is also used to freshen up garments that have recently been unpacked or are slightly creased from being in the wardrobe for a prolonged period. You can also use the steam button on your iron to create a jet of steam, as an alternative to an upright steamer.

Fill the steamer with water and wait for it to heat up. Hang the garment on the upright rail part of the steamer or on a clothing rail – for longer garments, make sure the rail is high enough so that the dress hangs freely and you can reach every part of it. Do not hang it on the back of a door or on other furniture as you will risk damaging these with the steam.

Ensure you are working in a well-ventilated area to minimise the risk of setting off smoke/fire alarms. When the steam starts to appear, run the nozzle of the steamer over the garment, starting at the bottom and moving upwards. Be careful not to drip water onto the garment from the condensation caused by the steamer.

You can touch the garment with the steamer nozzle, but for delicate fabrics such as silk, hover the nozzle of the steamer above the fabric and the steam produced will quickly eliminate creases. Delicate beaded or embroidered garments should be steamed inside out. Do not overfill the steamer, and monitor the water level so that you can refill it before it runs out.

Top tip

If you find yourself in a hotel with a crumpled dress and no iron, try filling the bathroom with steam from a hot shower and hang your dress up nearby – the temporary sauna effect will help to relax clothing creases.

Stain removal

The stains could be seen only in the sunlight ...
The alcohol had the effect of making the
black cloth blacker. This amused her; she had
noted in her journal: 'booze affects material as
it does people'.

THE LOVELY BONES, ALICE SEBOLD

The most frequent clothing crisis you are likely to come across is stain removal. Even if you have the dining etiquette of a duchess, your clothes will at some point fall victim to a splash of sauce or a dribble of gravy. The word 'stain' conveys a measure of permanence; most everyday stains on clothing can be removed effectively, however, if dealt with swiftly. Timing is of the essence – if left to dry before taking action, the stain will begin to settle into the fibres of the garment and become more difficult to remove. Always treat stains before washing, as heat and soap could fix the stain, making it harder to remove. You may have to wash the garment more than once, or try a different product, but most stains will disappear eventually. The important thing is not to panic if an expensive item gets stained as this will only make it worse.

Stain removal products

Stain removal products work by either dissolving the stain in a solvent, or creating a chemical reaction to break down the ingredients; for example, enzymes in a biological detergent break down the proteins in blood to eliminate the stain. So it is important that the product you choose contains the right solvent/agent to dissolve or break down the constituents of the stain. See Appendix I for a list of commercial products that are useful to have in the house, ready for stain emergencies. Always follow the directions on the manufacturer's label. Stain Devils are good products to have in your laundry 'first-aid kit' as they are designed to target specific stains and are suitable for delicate fabrics. Vanish is a popular and effective universal stain removal pre-wash treatment, but it is only suitable for cottons and some synthetics, not delicates.

Pre-wash treatment

Most everyday food stains can be treated with a pre-wash product, which you either apply directly onto the fabric, or dissolve in cool water and allow the stained item to soak. Often all that is needed with food stains on most fabrics is a quick spray of pre-wash treatment followed by a normal wash, and the stain will be gone. This is the gentlest way of treating the fabric. Garments that are heavily stained should be pre-soaked with an enzyme-based product such as Vanish, if they are made of textiles suitable for soaking, such as cotton, but do not soak delicate items, such as silk and wool. Use a plastic bowl as you would for hand-washing, and make sure the detergent is thoroughly dissolved before adding the garment to soak. Garments should be left to soak for at least an hour, several if possible; whites can be left overnight. For tricky stains, try rubbing the detergent directly into the stain before soaking. With drink spillages, the key is to blot as much of the liquid as possible to prevent it drying, and then apply an appropriate pre-wash treatment.

Spot treatments

Stain removal spot treatments, such as Stain Devils, are the next step up from a pre-wash treatment and involve targeting the stained area directly with a solvent specially formulated to fight the stain's specific ingredients. This treatment is advisable for stubborn stains, such as red wine and coffee.

Stain removal steps

• With solid stains, scrape off any excess with a knife.
• Lay the garment on a towel or kitchen paper right side down while treating the stain, to absorb any excess moisture. Move to a different area of the towel as soon as it becomes dirty, to prevent re-staining the garment.
• Blot the stain with white kitchen paper to remove excess moisture. Do not rub. Use a cotton bud for small stains on delicate fabrics.
• Keep replacing the kitchen paper/cotton buds as soon as they get dirty, to prevent pushing the stain back on to the fabric.
• Apply cool water to loosen the particles of the stain, and blot again.
• Apply a pre-wash treatment to the area; repeat on the reverse of the fabric. Leave for a few minutes.
• Wash as normal, according to fabric type. Cotton: wash at 40 degrees using a biological detergent to boost the cleaning power. Silks, wools and delicates: machine wash at 30 degrees using a liquid detergent suitable for delicates and on a delicates programme, or hand-wash.
• If the stain is still present, repeat the process, leaving the treatment on for a longer time.
• Once eliminated, allow the garment to dry naturally.

Types of stain

There are three main types of stain: pigment, protein and grease, each requiring slightly different approaches for effective removal. Below is a guide to the different types of stains, with some examples and the recommended general treatment. This treatment is for washable fabrics, such as cotton/linen and polyester. For delicate fabrics, such as wool and silk, see Delicate Fabrics on page 137.

Pigment-based stains

Examples: Coloured products and food, e.g. wine, coffee, tea, fruit juice, perfume, grass, ink.

Treatment: Blot stain with kitchen paper. Flush with cold water and blot again. Follow with a pre-soak using a biological pre-wash treatment powder, e.g. Vanish Platinum Oxi-Action Powder, or apply a gel treatment directly to the stain, e.g. Vanish Gold Pre-Treat Power Gel. Leave for five to ten minutes and then wash according to the fabric type. For very bad stains add another scoop of Vanish powder to the wash – the bleaching agents will continue to fight the stain in the washing machine. If the stain is still present, try again with a suitable spot treatment, such as Stain Devils Tea, Red Wine and Fruit and Juice.

Notes to remember: For tannin-based stains, such as wine, tea and coffee, never use salt or soap to treat the stain – both will set the tannin stain permanently.

Protein-based stains

Examples: Most food stains, e.g. egg, milk, chocolate. Sweat, blood.

Treatment: Lift any excess solid matter with a blunt knife.

Blot with paper towel. Soak in cold water. Add a biological pre-soaking agent. The enzymes within this product will break down the amino acids within the protein stain. Then machine wash at 40 degrees using a biological detergent. If the stain is still present, try again with a spot treatment, e.g. Stain Devils Blood and Dairy.

Notes to remember: Never use hot water to remove these stains – the protein can coagulate and set into the fibres of the textiles. Do not use biological pre-soaking agents and bio detergents on delicate fabrics such as silks and wools.

Grease-based stains

Examples: Butter, oil, mayonnaise, suntan lotion.
Treatment: Scrape off solid parts. Soak up excess moisture with kitchen paper. Sprinkle with baking powder or baby powder to absorb the oil. Shake off and apply liquid detergent to the area, then leave for a few minutes. Machine wash according to fabric type. If the stain is still present, try Stain Devils for Cooking Oil and Fat.

Combination stains

Combination stains have more than one component, e.g. lipstick contains grease and pigment. For this type of stain, treat the protein/grease ingredient first, as above, and then follow with a treatment for pigment-based stains, if needed.

Delicate fabrics

Delicate fabrics, such as silk and wool, should never be soaked or washed at high temperatures. Most stain-removal products cannot be used on silk and wool, as the delicate fibres are liable to suffer damage and discolouration from the solvents within the stain removers. Start by just blotting and gently rinsing with cold water; if the stain is not fading, apply a little neat distilled white vinegar in small amounts using a cotton bud. Take extra care when treating delicate fabrics such as silk, which becomes weak when wet so should not be rubbed, as you will risk damaging the fibres (as well as making the stain worse). Although silk should not be soaked, it should always be washed after stain removal, as even water can leave permanent stain marks. Hand-wash or machine wash on a delicates cycle using a liquid detergent suitable for delicate fabrics. Do not use biological detergents on silks and wools; these fibres contain protein, so the fibres will be damaged by the enzymes in the bio detergent. For expensive/dry-clean only fabrics, it is best to apply a little 'first aid' in terms of blotting, and then get it to a specialist dry-cleaner as soon as possible. Make sure you tell them what the origin of the stain is, to increase the chances of effective removal.

Stain removal – dos and don'ts

- **DON'T** initially treat stains with hot water – it will set the stain.
- **DON'T** allow a fabric to dry or iron it after washing if it is still stained – the heat will set the stain. Repeat the treatment and wash until the stain disappears.
- **DO** test stain removal products on a hidden part of brightly coloured garments, e.g. the hem, to ensure that the solvent does not remove any fabric dye.
- **DON'T** pre-soak silks and other delicate fabrics. Use a spot treatment suitable for delicates.
- **DO** work from the outside in when applying the stain remover to large stains, to avoid spreading the stain.
- **DO** always dab the stain – **DON'T** rub (especially on delicate fabrics) as this will spread the stain and damage the fabric.
- **DO** be patient – **DON'T** flood the stain with product; apply in small amounts and repeat the process if necessary.

Top tip

For stain removal 'on the go', add a portable stain removal product to your handbag or suitcase (such as a pocket stain removal wipe or pen). See Appendix I for useful addresses/products.

Sticky stains

Chewing gum

Place the garment in the freezer for a few hours. The gum will become brittle and easier to pick off with a blunt knife. If the garment is too large (or the freezer too small), place an ice pack over the area until the gum hardens. Once the gum is removed, apply a little pre-wash treatment to the area, such as De-Solv-It Sticky Stuff Remover, and then wash according to fabric type.

Candle wax

Place the garment on an ironing board with a piece of greaseproof paper over the affected area. Glide a warm iron gently over the surface of the paper – the wax will melt and stick to the greaseproof paper. Apply a little Sticky Stuff Remover to the fabric and then wash according to fabric type.

Natural stain removers

• **Distilled white vinegar** is a very effective, cheap and environmentally friendly agent for stain removal. Its acetic acid component is a natural bleaching agent. Use neat as a spot treatment, or diluted with water to pre-soak garments before washing. White vinegar also has softening properties, so is a natural alternative to fabric softener.
• **Baking soda** is very useful for grease-based stains – sprinkle over the stain and leave for an hour to absorb the excess moisture. With other types of stain (if the fabric is strong, like a white cotton T-shirt), mix the powder into a paste using a 2:1 ratio with water, and scrub over the fabric with a toothbrush as a pre-treatment to washing.

Common clothing crises

Shrunken knitwear

Wool should always be hand-washed at a cool temperature and never tumble-dried – excess heat will cause the fibres, and thus the garment, to shrink. The results can be quite startling, but fear not – if your precious woollen knits accidentally creep into a hot wash or tumble-drier, there is a way of reversing the shrinkage, if dealt with straight away. It may still be a little snug, but it should stretch back into adult-wear size rather than being relegated to a child's wardrobe. Remember when washing knitwear to always re-shape while still damp, as even when washed correctly at a cool temperature, the natural fibres will shrink slightly until re-shaped.

• **Fill a plastic bowl** or sink with lukewarm water and add a capful of delicates liquid detergent (e.g. Woolite).
• **Agitate the jumper** in the solution gently to allow the detergent to enter the weave and relax the fibres.
• **Leave to soak** for about 15–20 minute and then rinse.
• **Remove from the water** and gently squeeze to eliminate excess water (do not wring).
• **Place on a flat towel** and roll up to remove excess moisture.
• **While still damp**, place on another towel and gently stretch the jumper to re-shape. Natural fibres such as wool are very pliable when wet, so they should slowly regain their original shape.
• **Leave to dry naturally**; check and re-stretch at regular intervals before the garment is completely dry.

Bobbly jumpers

A common clothing complaint is bobbling or pilling of knitwear, which can make jumpers look worn and weary. Pilling is where the textile fibres break up and form little fuzzy bobbles. It is a result of daily wear and will be most noticeable in areas where the garment rubs against your skin (such as under the arms or elbows), or where the knitwear rubs against another layer of fabric (such as under a coat). It is usually most visible after washing, as the washing-machine agitation will add to the aggravation of these broken fibres. Both natural and synthetic knitwear is prone to pilling, but it is more common with garments made of looser and soft fibres, such as cashmere and mohair or mixed-fibre blends.

To minimise pilling, wash vulnerable knitwear inside out by hand, using a delicates liquid detergent and only when necessary – over-washing will hasten any damage (see Hand-washing on page 125). If washing by machine, choose a delicates cycle that will lessen the agitation of the

knitwear in the drum. Avoid using fabric softeners when washing knitwear; these will soften the fibres making them more susceptible to becoming loose and forming a bobble. Consider also what type of jacket or coat you wear over delicate knits like cashmere – if you wear an unlined coat, for instance, or a rough denim jacket, then this is going to be very abrasive against the soft knit and will hasten the appearance of bobbles.

Brush your knitwear gently after wear, using a natural bristle brush for clothes – this will smoothen the beginnings of any loose ends while also removing dust and lint, keeping the jumper fresh and lessening the need for washing. A knitwear de-pilling comb is the best tool for removing bobbles on delicate knits. Mechanical jumper razors will also trim the bobbles effectively, but take care if using these as you risk damaging the good fibres within jumpers if you are too rough. Brush the jumper with a clothing brush after de-pilling to remove any stray fibres. Don't pull on the bobble by hand as you will loosen the fibres further and weaken the yarn.

Brighten dull sneakers

White canvas sneakers are an excellent wardrobe footwear staple, but with daily wear comes the accumulation of daily grime, which is more noticeable on white shoes. For small marks, try using a Mr Clean Magic Eraser (available online) – these white spongy blocks are generally used for erasing stains around the home, such as on doors, light switches and skirting boards, but they also work well on white sneakers – just add a little water and rub on the shoe to erase the stain – it works better on the rubber edging of the shoe. For sneakers with more built-up grime, wash either by hand or in the washing machine, to revitalise them and retrieve their white glow. Washing sneakers in the machine is okay occasionally, and on a short cycle, but not too regularly as the agitation from the machine and the full immersion in water for lengthy periods of time will naturally contribute to the deterioration of the shoe structure.

Hand-washing sneakers

• Remove the laces from the shoe and treat with stain remover – they are likely to be grubby around the points where the lace has been inserted into the metal-rimmed lace holes of the shoe. If they are very bad, leave to soak in a bowl of warm water with a bleaching agent (e.g. Vanish) for a couple of hours.

• Apply a mild liquid detergent to the shoe (washing-up liquid or a delicates liquid detergent) and use a toothbrush to gently scrub the shoe. Dip in a bowl of warm water to rinse and repeat until the stains have gone. For added bleaching power, add a teaspoon of Vanish powder or baking soda to the detergent before scrubbing on the shoe. If the stains are very bad, apply a pre-treatment stain removal product and then repeat the process.

- Rinse with clean water to remove all detergent and leave to dry naturally, in sunlight if possible to benefit from the sun's natural bleaching rays.
- Stuff with kitchen paper while they are drying to maintain their shape and absorb moisture (do not use newspaper – the print will transfer to the shoe).

Machine washing sneakers

- Remove laces and pre-treat as above before.
- Pre-treat grubby stains on the shoe. You can use a stain removal pre-treatment gel product such as Vanish, or make a paste with baking soda, mild detergent and water, scrubbing this into the shoe using an old toothbrush. Leave for up to an hour, if possible, depending on how grubby they are, and then follow with a machine wash.
- Place the sneakers into a mesh laundry bag or a cotton pillowcase to protect them. Hangerworld sell a padded mesh bag specifically for machine washing sneakers. You might also want to add a couple of old towels into the wash, to cushion the thud of the spinning sneakers in the machine drum. Wash on a cool delicates cycle and leave to air dry naturally, filling with kitchen paper as above.

Back to black – reviving faded jeans

Jeans as we know them have been a steadfast separate since they were first created by Levi Strauss and Jacob Davis in 1873. Conceived as a solution to a customer's request for a durable pair of trousers, they have evolved over the decades to reach iconic status as one of the most popular and practical wardrobe staples for all ages and seasons. They are likely to be one of the most worn garments in your wardrobe – and with frequent wear

Top tip

If your black jeans have faded, try dyeing with Dylon 'Wash & Dye' – this is a machine-friendly fabric dye that can be added to the washing machine to dye the denim. After dyeing, wash the jeans again with a Dylon Colour Catcher and a cup of white vinegar in the rinse cycle. The colour catcher will absorb any excess dye on the jeans and the white vinegar will set the dye and clean the machine. Run the machine on empty with a cup of white vinegar afterwards – and check the door of the machine for any black residue.

comes frequent washing, which, eventually, will lead to colour fading. Jeans are made of strong cotton denim, which is durable, but the dye used to colour the fabric is much more vulnerable. Jeans are at risk of more rapid fading than other coloured garments due to the way denim yarn is dyed by manufacturers – the dye doesn't penetrate the core of the denim fibres, only the outer surface, which makes jeans prone to colour transfer when new. Some people like the effect of faded blue denim over time, but with black jeans, colour intensity is often preferred. If you're a jean queen and live in denim, then it is worthwhile knowing how to properly care for your denim-wear in order to prolong its life.

Top tips for denim care and retaining colour in your wardrobe

• Apply a fabric protector to new jeans, such as Scotchguard. This will lock in the colour and delay fading whilst also repelling stains.

• Wash only when dirty to preserve the original dye for as long as possible. You can steam the denim to freshen it, or spray with fabric refresher.

• Use a detergent specifically tailored for coloured clothing to help retain colour intensity.

• Wash inside out – turning clothes inside out will protect the outer side from fading and friction within the machine.

• Wash in cool water – heat will contribute to colour fading.

• Wash on a short cycle – less time in the water means less time for colour leakage.

• Use white vinegar in the rinse cycle when washing – it will help to retain colour and eliminate any excess soap residue.

• Do not tumble-dry as this will damage the fabric – allow to dry naturally but not in direct sunlight, as this will bleach colour.

• Take care with stain removal on denim – do not attempt to rub out the stain, as you are likely to rub out the dye too. Pre-treat as you would a delicate fabric and wash as normal.

TRUST IS A MUST

> *Reflect then, seriously, before temptation lead you*
> *astray: reflect that when once you break through*
> *the barrier of good principle, it is difficult, if not*
> *impossible for you, ever to return.*

THE DUTIES OF A LADY'S MAID, ANON.

One of the main reasons such emphasis was placed on character and trust in advertisements for ladies' maids was due to the responsibility for and proximity to their mistress's valuable possessions – namely her jewels. Ladies' maids such as Rose and Hilda were entrusted with the key to their mistress's safe. This was a huge responsibility and an anxiety for them, as they would have to account for any missing items. They might also be requested to collect the most valuable items from the bank or transport cases of jewellery from one residence to another. While some ladies' maids gained the trust of their employer before going off the rails, there were also cases of young women falsifying references in order to gain employment as a lady's maid purely with the goal of stealing jewels from the lady of the house. In 1934, Kathleen Preston, a lady's maid, working in Mayfair, was sentenced to 15 months' imprisonment with hard labour for the theft of two brooches valued at £2,500 (almost £160,000 in today's money) from her employer. Preston obtained the job using a false reference from a Cornish schoolmistress, who was fined for providing the inaccurate testimony. Elsewhere, lady's maid Catherine Mary Macaulay gained 'the implicit confidence and trust' of her employer Lady Diana Worthington before being sentenced to three months' imprisonment with hard labour in 1932 for also stealing her mistress's jewels.

THE CONVICT LADY'S MAID

(From the Hertford Reformer, 1835)

A most singular event has occurred in the family of a noble Lord, which, however, unpleasant to the feelings of the parties concerned, it will be impossible long to keep from the knowledge of the public. We have, therefore, no scruple in stating what we heard respecting it.

Lady B. having lost some jewels last week, in the same mysterious way in which other robberies of a similar kind have been committed, sent for two police-officers to institute a rigorous inquiry amongst the domestics of the establishment.

The only individual whom her Ladyship proposed to exempt from personal search was her own maid, of whose integrity and excellent qualities, although she had been with her but a few months, Lady B entertained so high an opinion that she could not bear the idea of treating her as a object of suspicion. The offers arrived, and after a very short visit came at once to the astonished Lady B., and told her, "Madam, not only must your maid be searched, but she is the only person here who need be searched, for the maid has got your jewels, and what is more, the maid is man!" The fact was soon proved to the satisfaction of all.

The maid was a returned convict, a young man sentenced to transportation for life for various ingenious robberies, but who had made his escape, and assumed female apparel as the best mode of returning to this country with impunity. Of his extraordinary dexterity no better proof can be given than the fact that for eight months he had lived in Lady B.'s family without the slightest suspicion being entertained as to his sex, and had won the confidence of his mistress by the uniform propriety of his conduct. The affair is a very awkward one, and we really do not know what precautions ladies must take in future when forced to change their personal attendants. We pity Lady B. most sincerely for the very painful situation in which she has been placed, and wish it were possible to guard effectually against similar imposition.

Caring for cashmere

I embrace the colder weather as it is an opportunity to luxuriate in cosy cashmere sweaters. But the delicate nature of cashmere wool requires extra special care to keep it in tip-top condition that will see you through the winter this season, and many seasons to come.

Cashmere is a very fine, natural-hair fibre obtained from goats. Garments made of cashmere are much softer than lambswool and tend to be much more expensive. Its smoothness also makes it more wearable against the skin than lambswool. There is guidance below on how best to wash, dry and store cashmere, to prevent damaging its delicate fibres.

Washing

• When washing cashmere, turn the garment inside out and gently hand-wash in cool/lukewarm water and a gentle liquid detergent suitable for hand-washing (e.g. Woolite) or a specialist cashmere shampoo.
• Make sure that the detergent is dissolved thoroughly in the water before adding the clothing (add hot water first to dissolve the detergent and then top up with cold water to achieve a cool temperature).
• Use a gentle squeezing movement, rather than rubbing, which can cause felting and damage the fibres.
• Rinse in cool water to remove all traces of the detergent.

Drying

• Never tumble-dry cashmere (or any wool garment), as this will shrink the garment.
• Do not wring dry as this will cause structural damage to the fibres.
• Gently squeeze after rinsing and then roll in a clean towel to remove excess moisture; and leave to dry flat on a soft dry towel.
• Re-shape while damp to maintain the shape of the garment.
• Do not hang on a hanger to dry as this will stretch the garment.

Storing

Cashmere knitwear is best kept folded in your wardrobe or drawers to prevent the delicate fibres from stretching on clothes hangers. Some finer knitwear can be hung on hangers to prevent creasing, but make sure that you use suitable hangers that protect the shoulder area as much as possible.

When storing cashmere garments long term, protect them from pests by packing in a special knitwear bag or in a similar breathable clothing bag. See Seasonal Storage on page 109 for further tips on storing clothes.

The scourge of the moth

The old definition of moth was, 'anything that gradually, silently eats, consumes, or wastes any other thing.' It was a verb for destruction too …

THE SILENCE OF THE LAMBS, THOMAS HARRIS

There is one creature that really tests my otherwise impeccable and unflappable professional demeanour, and that is the clothes moth. It indiscriminately wreaks havoc within the finest of wardrobes across the land, ravaging the most expensive and luxurious of clothing. So what should one do if one's winter woollens fall victim to the scourge of the dreaded moth? If your winter wardrobe is full of cosy cashmere and luxury knitwear, then I applaud you for your excellent taste, but unfortunately the moth has exquisite taste to match. In fact, the finer the yarn, the more digestible it is; so angora and cashmere are akin to banquet food for moths. Clothing made of animal

protein fibres only, such as silk, wool and leather, are the textiles most at risk from moth attack. The damage itself is not caused by the adult moth but by the larvae that the female moths produce. These larvae burrow across protein fibres within the textile, eating it as they go and leaving behind holes in the fabric. It is worth mentioning here that the type of moths that cause trouble in your wardrobe are the common clothes moth and the case-bearing clothes moth, which are generally smaller and paler in colour, compared to the large brown house moths that you may find flying kamikaze-style into your bedside lamp. These larger house moths prefer feeding on plant material, so are not a threat to your wardrobe.

Recognising a moth attack

Clothes moths live quite happily in warm and dark areas, so you may not even notice that you have a problem until you bring out your winter clothing after storing it for the summer months. If you notice large, ragged holes in your knitwear, then this is probably the result of a moth attack. Other signs could be the presence of little eggs about the size of a pin-head; these then hatch into larvae, which look like creamy white caterpillars. They then feed on the clothing fibres, leaving behind trails that look similar to wispy cobwebs.

Top tips for treating a moth infestation

• Remove all clothing from wardrobes, even if it isn't visibly damaged. Wash or dry-clean to kill any moth eggs or larvae that may be present on the clothing. Brushing clothing or ironing with a hot iron (between a damp pressing cloth, if necessary) will also destroy moth eggs.

• Thoroughly vacuum and clean the wardrobe and room, paying particular attention to the cracks and crevices of the wardrobe and the corners of the room, in case any moths are hiding under carpets. Dispose of the vacuum bag immediately as this will be a dream home for moths – if you have sucked up any larvae, they will set up residence inside the bag.

• To trap adult male moths and prevent them from breeding, place a pheromone moth trap inside the bedroom/dressing room. The strip contains powder saturated with female pheromones, which will attract and trap the male moths, preventing them from reproducing and causing any further damage.

• For clothing that is damaged, isolate the garment by placing in a cellophane bag and then into a freezer for two to three days. This will kill any moth eggs or larvae that may be present. On removal from the freezer, leave the garment in the bag until it is brought back to room temperature.

• If the holes are not too big, it may be possible to repair damaged woollen garments by darning. If the damage is very bad and the garment is valuable to you, take it to a professional to repair. There is a process called 'invisible mending', where threads are taken from the seam allowance of the garments and re-woven over the hole by hand (see Appendix I for useful addresses).

• If the infestation is bad, consider using a pesticide spray such as Moth Stop Spray (available from Lakeland). Spray over infested areas of the house, paying particular attention to the cracks and crevices of the units.

Top tip

Always wash or dry-clean clothes before long-term storage and pack away properly to minimise the risk of attracting moths (see Seasonal Storage on page 109). Pay particular attention to clothing that is made of protein fibres, such as wool, feather, leather or silk.

• Remember never to spray pesticides directly onto clothing – all clothing should be removed from the wardrobe before any pesticide is used.

• If, after returning your clothing to the wardrobe, you notice further insect damage, it may be necessary to seek help from a pest control professional to treat the infestation.

Preventing future moth attacks

Keep your house as clean and dust-free as possible – vacuum and dust regularly, especially around the wardrobe space and clothing storage areas. The wardrobe itself should be cleaned out thoroughly a couple of times a year – perhaps when you are rotating the clothes with the seasons. Re-line drawers with lavender or cedar-scented lining paper (see Appendix I for useful products/ addresses). Try to do a deep clean in the bedroom/dressing room two or three times a year to prevent a build-up of dust and dirt. Deep cleaning is a more thorough clean, where furniture is moved and cleaned underneath, inside and out. Every surface, nook and cranny is thoroughly dusted, cleaned and vacuumed. If you do this, then you should notice the early signs of moth presence before too much damage is done.

Moth deterrents

Prevention is always better than cure, and in the case of moths, it is possible to deter them by surrounding your clothing with a scent that repels them. Lavender sachets or cushions are a particular favourite as they are natural and will also make your clothes smell nice. Wooden cedar balls or blocks are equally repellent to the moth. (See Appendix I for stockists.) Add a few hanging lavender sachets to your wardrobe, and place a sachet or two in your drawers on top of vulnerable knitwear. Replace or refill every season, or whenever the smell starts to fade, as their moth-repelling properties will wear off over time. Some hanging sachets are available with a built-in indicator that tells you when it needs to be replaced. If you are handy with a needle and thread, you could make your own lavender sachets using scraps of fabric and dried lavender.

Care of accessories

Shoes

Shoes should always be stored with either shoe trees inside, shoe puffs (padded shoe inserts) or rolled-up acid-free tissue paper to maintain their shape. If shoes are not kept in boxes, give them a dust when you are cleaning the room. To prolong the life of the upper part of the shoe, always apply a protective spray when new, keep clean and condition now and then to maintain the material. Do not allow the cap on the tip of the heel to wear down too far, or the sole to get too worn, as you will risk damage to the rest of the shoe. Check the soles and heels, if worn regularly, and take to a cobbler to re-sole or re-heel.

Leather shoes

Apply leather protector when new to protect from water damage. Clean shoes when necessary with appropriate shoe polish to maintain the colour and condition. Leather conditioner will also help keep shoes and other leather garments in good condition. Conditioner is different from polish as it is colourless, so can be used on all leather colours and types. If leather shoes get wet, never leave to dry next to artificial heat, which could crack the leather and damage the shoe. Stuff the toe with kitchen paper to absorb excess moisture and allow to dry naturally before cleaning. If shoes have a leather sole, these will be porous when wet, so consider getting them fitted with a rubber sole, or protect the sole with a product such as Sole Guard (available from Russell & Bromley).

How to polish leather shoes

Make sure the surface of the shoe is clean and dry by wiping with a clean cloth before polishing. Pick a suitable leather polish according to the colour of the shoes. Apply the polish in small amounts using a yellow duster and a circular polishing motion. Buff with a bristle brush suitable for leather shoes, or with a duster. Shoe-shine sponges are available; these are ideal for a quick buff of leather shoes if they are in need of a shine and you don't have time for a full-on polish (see Appendix I for details).

• **Ballet shoes.** Hand-wash in a bowl as you would delicate silks, using a mild liquid detergent and cool water. Dab with a towel to remove excess moisture and allow to dry naturally on a soft towel.

• **Canvas shoes.** Some canvas shoes can be washed in the washing machine – place in a lingerie mesh bag to prevent agitation in the machine. Wash on a low programme, as for synthetics or delicates. Otherwise use a shoe shampoo cleaner suitable for fabric shoes, or a mild delicates detergent. See Brighten Dull Sneakers, page 143.

• **Nubuck leather shoes.** Nubuck is similar to suede but has a finer pile. Use a specialist solvent-based cleaner. Do not use a suede cleaner or brush as this will damage the pile.

• **Patent leather shoes.** Dust patent leather shoes with a soft cloth. To revitalise, apply patent leather gloss product occasionally.

• **Pony hair shoes.** Use a protective spray and brush with a soft brush if they get dirty. Cleaning products are not recommended, but if necessary, clean carefully with a mild detergent/water solution.

• **Satin shoes.** Take extra care when wearing satin shoes as they are very tricky to clean. Cleaning products are not recommended, but if necessary, clean carefully with a mild detergent/water solution and a cotton bud on the stained area.

• **Suede shoes.** Treat new shoes with a suede protector spray. Brush regularly after use with a suede brush to remove dust and raise the pile. Remove marks using a suede block. If necessary, clean with a brush dipped in soapy water or a specialist suede cleaner. If they get wet, fill with rolled-up kitchen paper and allow to dry naturally.

• **Trainers.** Wipe with a cloth soaked in a mild detergent solution. Do not leave in a sports kit bag if damp as mould will form. See Machine Washing Sneakers, page 145.

• **Velvet shoes.** Use a lint roller or rolled-up sticky tape to remove dust and fluff. If cleaning is necessary, dab with soapy water and allow to dry naturally.

Boots

Clean boots as you would shoes, according to fabric type, and store with boot shapers inside to maintain the shape of the boot and prevent creasing.

• **Ugg boots and similar.** Sheepskin – brush to revive the appearance. Clean with mild soapy water or a specialist sheepskin cleaner. Do not saturate the sheepskin with water as this will matt the fur. Allow to dry naturally.

• **Wellies.** Protect with a silicone spray protector. Wash with soapy water and dry with a cloth. Leave to dry naturally and thoroughly, away from direct heat. Store in a cool, dry, well-ventilated place – extreme temperatures will crack the rubber, especially if it isn't protected with silicone. If white 'bloom' marks appear, wipe with a warm damp cloth and use a specialist boot-cleaning product to remove the marks (see Appendix I for useful addresses).

Bags

• **Leather bags.** Apply leather protector when new to protect from water and stains. If the bag gets dirty, wipe with a damp cloth. Leather bags do not need much ongoing maintenance, besides filling with tissue paper when not in use to maintain their shape. They can be occasionally conditioned with a leather maintainer cream, but don't use any pigmented conditioners aimed at shoe leather as they might rub off on clothing.

• **Canvas bags.** Some can be machine washed – refer to the label and wash as you would canvas shoes. Otherwise, most synthetic fabric bags should be cleaned by wiping with a damp cloth.

Gloves

• **Leather gloves.** Hand-wash with a mild soap such as baby shampoo in lukewarm water. Don't rub the leather but press gently. After rinsing, press with a towel to remove excess moisture. Blow into the gloves to help regain the natural form, and then hang to dry away from direct heat. If you have a glove form to leave them on to dry, even better.

- **Suede gloves.** See care of suede shoes, p. 159.
- **Woollen/cotton/silk gloves.** Hand-wash using a mild liquid detergent suitable for delicate fibres. Press with a towel to remove excess moisture, re-shape while damp and allow to dry naturally on a soft towel. Iron when dry using a pressing cloth.

Hats

- **Panama/straw hats.** Always fill the crown and wrap in acid-free tissue paper and store in a hatbox when not in use or when travelling, in order to maintain the shape. If the brim or crown gets bent, apply steam from a steam iron or portable steamer and gently mould the hat until the original shape returns. If the hat is badly misshapen, take to a specialist hatter who can re-block the hat (stretch it back to its original shape using a wooden block; see Appendix I).
- **Felt hats.** Brush after wear with a natural bristle brush to remove dust and dirt. Apply steam from a steam iron or portable steamer to smooth and freshen. If the hat gets wet, remove excess moisture with a clean, absorbent cloth and then leave to air dry naturally, away from direct heat. Line and wrap in acid-free tissue paper and store in

a hatbox when not in use or when travelling in order to maintain the shape.

- **Tweed hats.** Brush after wear with a natural bristle brush to remove dust and dirt. Apply steam from a steam iron or portable steamer to smooth and freshen. Tweed caps can be rolled when travelling – but remember to unroll and re-shape on arrival.
- **Faux fur hats.** Use a soft bristle hat brush to revive and remove dust.
- **Woollen hats.** Hand-wash as you would a woollen jumper – re-shape when damp and dry naturally.

Sunglasses and glasses

Sunglasses are likely to need regular cleaning due to a build-up of make-up and hairspray residues and other natural skin and hair oils. For on-the-go cleaning, use a microfibre lens cloth, either dry or with lens cleaner spray. Individual-use wet wipes are also available and are very handy for travel. Do not use other fabric, such as your clothing or tissues, to clean lenses as this will transfer dust/fluff on to the lenses and you'll also risk scratching them. Avoid breathing on lenses to clean them – this will spread any dirt or dust around rather than removing it. Every now and then, clean thoroughly by washing carefully with warm water and a drop of mild detergent, such as washing-up liquid. Rinse and dry with a lint-free cloth. Keep in the bag in which they came to prevent scratching to the lenses.

Jewellery care

I've never thought of my jewellery as trophies. I'm here to take care of it and to love it, for we are only temporary custodians of beauty.

ELIZABETH TAYLOR

To keep your jewellery in good condition, always remove it before you bathe or shower to minimise damage from water/soap. If you recognise that gemstones are losing their lustre, or dust or dirt has accumulated in the settings, then clean the pieces using the steps below as a guide. If in doubt about the identity of the gemstone or how to clean it, take it to a jeweller to be cleaned professionally. Some jewellers will offer a complimentary cleaning service for items bought in their store.

The guide below is for fine jewellery (precious metals and gemstones). Costume jewellery can be cleaned by brushing occasionally with a baby's toothbrush to dislodge dirt. Soap and water should be avoided for costume jewellery as it can leave a residue on the metal. If the jewellery has stones stuck on, the adhesive holding them is likely to be loosened by cleaning.

• **Gold and platinum** jewellery can be washed in lukewarm water with a drop of washing-up liquid (preferably unperfumed and colourless). Or you can buy a specialist jewellery cleaner from most jewellers. Do not wash if set with a porous stone such as pearls (see below).

• **Diamonds, sapphires, rubies, garnets, amethysts** and other transparent gemstones (with the exception of emeralds and aquamarines) can be cleaned in a solution of lukewarm water with washing-up liquid.

• **Emeralds and aquamarines** are porous and softer than other gemstones, so chip easily. They are also sensitive to extremes in temperature. They can be cleaned in a solution of water and washing-up liquid, but take extra care – emeralds are often treated with oil, which will be removed if washed in water, so if in doubt, seek specialist advice from a jeweller.

• **Silver** can also be washed in the same way as gold or platinum. If tarnished, clean with a silver polishing cloth. Take extra care when cleaning silver set with porous

gemstones. Do not wash. If the silver polishing cloth doesn't remove the tarnish, use cotton buds dipped in silver polish. Use the tiniest amount and remove residue with another cotton bud dipped in water, making sure that neither the polish nor the water come into contact with the gemstone.

• **Pearls** should never be washed in water. Pearls benefit from the oils that human skin produces, so wearing them often will improve their lustre. Always put pearls on last, after applying make-up, perfume or hairspray, as these products could damage the pearl. Polish with chamois leather to improve their lustre. For pearl necklaces, check the string regularly; if it looks weak or you notice gaps widening between the pearls, have them re-strung before they break.

• **Opaque stones**, such as turquoise, coral, lapis lazuli and opals, are porous, so as with pearls, never wash in water. Polish with a soft cloth, such as a dry chamois leather cloth, and use a soft bristle brush (artist's paintbrushes are ideal) to clean the settings.

• **Opals** are similar to pearls in that their lustre will improve with regular wear. Both pearls and opals will begin to peel if kept in an atmosphere that is too dry.

Cleaning jewellery

When cleaning jewellery, always use a plastic bowl with a cloth at the bottom; do not wash in sinks in case pieces get lost down the plughole.

• Place each item in the bowl one at a time, leaving to soak for a few minutes to dislodge any dirt that is in the settings.

- If needed, brush each item gently with a small toothbrush, one at a time. Pay particular attention to rings, which have a tendency to accumulate dirt behind the stone.
- Rinse in lukewarm water and drain on paper towels or a dry tea towel.
- Once you have finished cleaning, remember to check the water bowl before discarding, in case any loose gemstones have escaped.
- Polish the items with a microfibre jewellery mitt or chamois leather. Take care not to use anything that could catch on the settings.

Storing jewellery

Jewellery should be stored in boxes to prevent damage from dust and humidity. Protect gems by storing in the jewellery boxes in which they came, or wrap in jewellery felt. Avoid storing items close together, to prevent the risk of scratching. Silver should be stored in silver-protecting cloths, to minimise tarnish. Pearls are easily scratched so should be kept in a soft felt pouch. Jewellery rolls are good for travel, but take care to protect expensive items by wrapping in acid-free tissue paper. If you use a large jewellery box, make sure each item is given enough space so that harder gems don't scratch softer metals. Fasten clasps on necklaces before putting away and keep earring pairs together. If chains become tangled, use a sewing needle to loosen the knots. Dusting with talcum powder can ease this process.

Hairbrushes and combs should be washed regularly to remove a build-up of hair products, hair oils and dust. Make-up brushes also require regular cleaning to remove the build-up of old make-up, dirt, bacteria and dust. Specialist brush-cleaning products are available, but a solution of water and washing-up liquid, hand soap or baby shampoo works just as well.

Hairbrushes
• Remove any excess hair from the bristles by running a comb through them.
• Do not immerse in water; clean by immersing only the bristles in a bowl containing a solution of lukewarm water and a little washing-up liquid.
• Rinse by dipping the bristles in plain water.
• Shake dry and dab with a soft towel to remove excess moisture.
• Leave to dry naturally.

Combs
• Soak in lukewarm water/washing-up liquid solution to remove dust and dirt.
• Use a toothbrush or nailbrush to clean gently between the teeth of the comb.
• Rinse in plain water and leave to dry naturally.
• Alternatively, you could use a solution of bicarbonate of soda and warm water: place a teaspoon of bicarb in a bowl of lukewarm water, soak the combs for about 15–20 minutes, and rinse. Bicarbonate of soda will absorb any oil present, as well as neutralising odours.

Make-up brushes

As you use make-up brushes directly on your face, these could cause spots or eye infections if not cleaned regularly.

• Use lukewarm water/washing-up liquid, or a water/ bicarbonate of soda solution, as above. Bicarbonate of soda will absorb any make-up residue or skin oils and will also get rid of any musty smells.

• Dip only the bristles in the water and avoid getting the ferrule and handles wet.

• Rub through the bristles to remove all the make-up; if using washing-up liquid, make a lather on your hand to rub the bristles through.

• Rinse in plain water and wrap with kitchen paper to remove excess moisture. Remove as much moisture as possible this way, as if left to air dry the bristles could lose their shape.

• Place flat on kitchen paper to dry naturally.

Sewing skills – Make Do and Mend

Mend clothes before washing them as the tear or hole may become unmanageable. Keep a look out for loose buttons and other fastenings and mend at once. Save all tapes, ribbons, buttons, hooks and eyes and keep a well-stocked work basket.

MAKE DO AND MEND, THE BRITISH MINISTRY OF INFORMATION

During the Second World War, the Government issued a pamphlet entitled *Make Do and Mend*, which offered women tips on how to be frugal with their clothing during times of hardship when clothing was rationed. During this time, people were strongly encouraged not to throw away anything if it could be fixed or used for something else. As new clothing was not easy to purchase, people naturally responded by caring for the clothes they had and making them last as long as possible. As well as offering advice on how to mend clothes, the pamphlet offered guidance on how to make new clothes out of old ones, or how to adapt menswear for women. The pamphlet was reissued and updated in 2007 for twenty-first-century families, to coincide with the economic recession.

Mending clothing was very common for families of the war generation and it is only recently that we have developed a 'throwaway' attitude to clothing; partly because, due to the cheap high-street clothing now available, people think it will be cheaper to buy new garments than to mend damaged ones. The idea of buying clothes to last, or 'handing down' to different generations, seems to have disappeared, along with the learning of domestic skills such as sewing. A little domestic knowledge will save you money in the long run, but you don't have to be an expert seamstress to fix a button or a hem – many garments can be saved once you learn a few basic sewing skills. You will also feel a sense of achievement knowing that you are spending time and effort fixing your clothes and prolonging their life, while resisting the easy way out of discarding and buying more. So if your favourite garment starts to suffer from wear and tear, don't despair or reach for the bin. If the damage is very bad and you feel it is beyond repair, then always dispose of clothing correctly (see Recycling Clothes on page 87).

Fixing damaged fabric will be easier if you notice it as soon as the damage occurs. Check clothes after wear to ensure that they are in good condition and are not damaged in any way. Pay particular attention to vulnerable areas, such as seams and hems, buttons, zips and other fastenings. As mentioned earlier, if you notice a problem, always repair it before washing, as the agitation of the machine will make the damage worse. The most common mending task will be sewing on a button, so try to keep any spares that come with garments so that you have an exact match, should the fallen button be lost.

Basic sewing kit

The following should be in every basic sewing kit to enable you to carry out minor repairs, such as sewing on a button or fixing a fallen hem.

• Needles
• Scissors (small scissors with pointed blades for snipping threads)
• Stitch ripper – to unpick seams

- Pins
- Tape measure
- An assortment of sewing threads
- Spare buttons

Needles

Sewing needles come in a range of sizes and thicknesses – make sure you use the correct one depending on the type of fabric you will be sewing: fabrics with a fine weave, like silk, will require sharp, thin needles, whereas thicker, blunt needles are more suitable for darning the loose weave of wool.

Sewing threads

Always choose a sewing thread with a fibre content similar to the fabric you will be sewing. Try to match the colour of the fabric as closely as possible. If a close match cannot be found, go for a slightly darker shade. Button thread is made from cotton-covered polyester. It is thick and strong and good for sewing on buttons. For tacking hems, use a contrasting colour of thread.

Have a look at a haberdashery department in a department store such as John Lewis for sewing supplies. For garments that are very damaged or very valuable, seek advice from a professional seamstress or textile conservator (see Appendix I).

Fastening off

Fastening off refers to the process of sealing the stitching to ensure that the thread does not unravel. When the area to be stitched has been completed, overstitch the last few stitches and then run the needle with the thread through the stitching or fabric several times, before finishing with a backstitch knot and snipping the thread as close to the fabric as possible.

Sewing a button

The stitches of those button-holes were so small – so small – they looked as if they had been made by little mice!

THE TAILOR OF GLOUCESTER, BEATRIX POTTER

When sewing a button onto a garment, use double-thickness thread or specialist button thread. If the fabric is of medium weight/thick material, create a shank when sewing on the button by following the steps below. This will give the buttonhole-side of the garment space to sit properly once the button is fastened.

• Mark the position where you want the button to be.
• Bring the needle through to the front of the fabric at this point.
• Pass the needle through one of the holes in the button. Lay a matchstick or toothpick across the centre of the button.
• Take the needle over the stick and down through the opposite hole and back through the fabric, trapping the matchstick. Repeat five times.
• Slide the stick out and bring the needle up beneath the button.
• Pull the button upwards.
• Wind the thread around the stitches underneath several times to form the stitched shank.
• Take the needle to the back and fasten off.

Hems

A common clothing casualty is the fallen hem; this is
fairly straightforward to fix by hand. If the garment is very
precious, then you may prefer to take it to a professional.

Fallen hems

• Start by pressing the hem, to ensure that it will be flat
when sewing.
• Secure the thread either side of the section where the
hem has come undone by unpicking a few stitches on
either side of the fallen section and fastening them off.
• Re-stitch the loose section using the method given below
for sewing a hem.

Hand-stitching a hem

• Using a ruler, measure the length of the hem required
while on the wearer, and mark with tailor's chalk or an
invisible pen. You can fold the hem and pin at this stage
to see how the garment hangs at this length, but it is best
to take the pins out once off the wearer, so that you can
press the hem before pinning again. If turning up trousers,
make sure you wear shoes when trying on the trousers.
• If the length that you need to remove is more than 1in
(2.5cm) for a double hem, you might want to cut off any
excess first before folding up the hem. (Do this off the
wearer and use fabric scissors.)
• You can make a single hem or double hem – double
hems give a firm edge, so are better for thicker fabrics.
For a double hem, first fold up the edge of the fabric by
³/₈ in (1cm), then press.
• Fold a second time, approximately ²/₃in (1.5cm), to
reach your required length. Press and pin in place.

• Tack with a straight running stitch using a thread of a contrasting colour.

• Remove pins.

• Using a matching thread, start at a seam line on the reverse side and make a tiny stitch through the edge of the hem; with the tip of the needle, pick up a couple of threads of the main fabric and a couple from the edge of the fold approximately 5mm to the left. Draw the thread through and repeat along the hem. This creates an invisible 'blind' stitch from the front of the fabric, so is the best stitch to use for hemming. Fasten off the thread through the hem and snip. Press again to finish.

Darning

Darning is the process of rebuilding a worn fabric using a weaving technique. Garments such as socks and sweaters are often darned to reinforce a weak area of the fabric or to seal a hole in the garment. The darning will be very visible, so it is especially important that the thread chosen is matched as closely as possible to the garment, in terms of colour, texture and fibre content. You will need a specific blunt needle for darning.

• Work on the inside of the garment.

• Do not fasten the thread on or off – leave the beginning and end stitch open so that the area to be mended blends in with the natural weave of the garment.

• Work quite loosely with the thread – keep the tension of the stitches even.

• Employing a running stitch, weave across the area to be darned, following the direction of the weave, and then reverse the needle and weave back at the end of the row.

• Leave a little loop at the end of each row to allow the threads space for movement.

The lady's maid's toolkit

- **Lint roller** – sticky paper roll, good for removing fluff, dust and hair from clothing.
- **Clothing brush** – natural bristle is better than synthetic. Good for general brushing of suits, knitwear and other clothing, to remove dust/dirt and to revive the pile.
- **Knitwear comb** to remove pilling on knitwear.
- **Acid-free tissue paper** for packing clothes into storage and protecting clothes.
- **Luggage labels** for identifying luggage and clothing bags.
- **Steam iron** – for most everyday ironing.
- **Upright steamer** – good for quickly removing creases on suits and dresses. Small portable steamers are great for travel.
- **Pressing cloth** – a plain, thin, soft white cotton cloth used for protecting delicate fabrics from excessive heat damage when ironing. Also prevents formation of shiny patches on knitwear when ironing.
- **Drying towels** – white cotton towels to use for drying garments that have been hand-washed.
- **Spray bottle** – used to re-dampen clothing to aid the ironing process.
- **Stain removal products**, e.g. Vanish, Stain Devils, baking soda, white vinegar.
- **Detergents suitable for different fabrics**, e.g. mild liquid detergent/bio and non-bio detergents/whiteners/colour retainers.
- **Mesh bag** for machine washing underwear or delicate fabrics, e.g. wool.
- **Portable clothing rail** – metal or wooden rail, can be adjustable. For wardrobe overflow or for planning travel wardrobes.
- **Lingerie bags** for packing underwear.

- **Dust bags (drawstring felt bags)** for packing shoes and handbags.
- **Folding template** – plastic template for folding knitwear and other tops, measuring approx. 14½ x 8²/₃in (37 x 22cm).
- **Knitwear storage bags** – breathable storage bags for storing woollen jumpers.
- **Lavender sachets** to refresh wardrobe areas and deter moths.
- **Sewing kit** – including different fibre threads (silk, cotton, etc.), a range of needles, pins, thread scissors, fabric scissors, stitch ripper, tape measure.
- **Jewellery/glasses cleaning kit** – lint-free cloth, microfibre lens cloth, lens cleaner, chamois leather cloth, cotton buds, silver jewellery cleaning cloth.
- **Shoe brushes and polish kit** – include polishes for different coloured leathers and different fabrics, such as canvas, cotton rags, dusters, shoe brushes, suede cleaning block. Leather/suede protector and maintainer.

www.theladysmaid.com
@theladysmaid

Bibliography

Anon., *The Duties of a Lady's Maid; with Directions for Conduct and Numerous Receipts for The Toilette* (Hampshire: Chawton House Press, 2015). Reproduced from *The Duties of a Lady's Maid* (London: Printed for James Bullock, 163, Strand, 1825).

Adams, Samuel and Sarah, *The Complete Servant* (London: Knight and Lacey, 1825).

Adlington, Lucy, *Stitches in Time: The Story of the Clothes We Wear* (London: Random House Books, 2016).

Baumgartner, Dr Jennifer, *You Are What You Wear: What Your Clothes Reveal About You* (Boston: Da Capo Press, 2012).

Bucar, Elizabeth, *Pious Fashion* (Cambridge, Massachusetts: Harvard University Press, 2017).

Campbell, Sophie, *The Season: A Summer Whirl Through the English Social Season* (London: Aurum Press Ltd, 2013).

Cassell's Household Guide (London: Cassell, Petter, and Galpin, 1869).

Coleno, Nadine, *The Hermès Scarf: History & Mystique* (London: Thames & Hudson, 2009).

Dean, Christina, Hannah Lane and Sofia Tärneberg, *Dress With Sense: The Practical Guide to a Conscious Closet* (London: Thames & Hudson Ltd, 2017).

Debrett's Handbook (London: Debrett's Ltd, 2014).

de Courcy, Anne, *1939: The Last Season* (London: Weidenfeld & Nicolson, 2003).

Harrison, Rosina, *The Lady's Maid: My Life in Service* (London: Ebury Press, 2011).

Kondo, Marie, *The Life-changing Magic of Tidying Up: The Japanese Art of Decluttering and Organizing* (London: Vermilion, 2011).

Lethbridge, Lucy, *Servants: A Downstairs View of Twentieth-century Britain* (London: Bloomsbury Publishing, 2013).

Make Do and Mend (London: Imperial War Museum; Facsimile edition, 2007). First published in London by the Ministry of Information in 1943.

Moyle, Anwyn, *Her Ladyship's Girl: A Maid's Life in London* (London: Simon & Schuster Ltd, 2014).

Newman, Hilda, *Diamonds at Dinner: My Life as A Lady's Maid in a 1930s Stately Home* (London: John Blake Publishing Ltd, 2013).

Singer Sewing Reference Library, *Sewing Essentials* (Minnetonka, Minnesota: Cy DeCosse Incorporated, 1984).

Stoney, Benita and Weltzien, Heinrich C. (eds), *My Mistress the Queen: The Letters of Frieda Arnold, Dresser to Queen Victoria* (London: Weidenfeld & Nicolson, 1994).

Taggart, Caroline, *Her Ladyship's Guide to the British Season* (London: National Trust Books, 2013).

Appendix I –
Useful addresses and products

Wardrobe organisation

The Holding Company – wardrobe storage solutions
Product range includes garment rails, clothing hangers, valet stands, drawer organisers, shoe storage, breathable mesh bags, vacuum storage bags, hatboxes. www.theholdingcompany.co.uk

Lakeland Ltd – wardrobe storage solutions, clothing and shoe-care products
Product range includes garment storage bags, shoeboxes, garment rails, moth repellents, clothing brushes and bobble shavers, mesh washing bags for laundry. Heated tower airers for line drying clothing. www.lakeland.co.uk

John Lewis – home department sells storage solutions, including garment bags, clothing rails, shoe racks and organisers, hangers, moth repellents. Haberdashery department sells sewing supplies. Also offers a service for made-to-measure wardrobes and other bedroom storage units. www.johnlewis.com

Hangerworld – storage solutions, underbed storage, clothing rails, garment covers, scented shoe puffs, moth deterrents, knitwear bags, lint removers and a wide range of hangers, including slimline velvet-coated hangers. Great for saving space. www.hangerworld.com

The White Company – homeware department sells clothing storage boxes and bags, drawer liners, moth repellents, wooden hangers. www.thewhitecompany.com

Muji – sells a wide range of transparent acrylic boxes; good for organising and displaying accessories such as costume jewellery and sunglasses. Also sells miniature bottles for dispensing travel toiletries. www.muji.com

Bespoke wardrobes

Neatsmith – London-based luxury bespoke wardrobes. www.neatsmith.co.uk

Wyndham Design – London-based bespoke wardrobes and bespoke storage solutions. www.wyndhamdesign.com

Spaceslide – sliding doors and made-to-measure wardrobes. Online design tool, so you can design and construct the wardrobe yourself. Installation service also available. www.spaceslide.co.uk

Ikea – Design your own affordable bespoke wardrobe space with Ikea's PAX wardrobes. You can design your own wardrobe in different sizes and styles to suit the size of your room and decor, and choose your own fittings to suit what you wear. Assembly service available. www.ikea.com

Shoe bags, laundry bags, lingerie bags

Monogrammed linen shop – monogrammed lingerie cases, laundry bags and shoe bags. www.monogrammedlinenshop.com

Cath Kidston – lingerie travel bags and shoe bags. www.cathkidston.com

Cashmere care

Brora – cashmere specialist selling a range of products to care for cashmere, including zip bags for storing jumpers, cashmere shampoo, cedar balls and cashmere combs for de-pilling. Stores nationwide. www.brora.co.uk

Pure Collection – jumper storage bags, cedar balls, cashmere shampoo, de-pilling combs. Stores nationwide. www.purecollection.com

Johnstons of Elgin – cedar balls, cashmere shampoo, de-pilling combs. Stores worldwide. www.johnstoncashmere.com

Modest clothing

The Modist – a new online store dedicated to dressing modestly; selecting the best pieces from contemporary luxury labels. www.themodist.com

Haute Elan – online store with a large range of stylish *abayas* and other modest clothing. www.haute-elan.com

East – Eastern-inspired British label with a variety of modest clothing options. www.east.co.uk

Moth prevention

USEFUL PRODUCTS

Lavender sachets – John Lewis, Lakeland, Boots, Cologne & Cotton, L'Occitane. John Lewis also sells knitwear storage bags scented with lavender.

www.lavenderworld.co.uk – sells dried lavender grown in North Yorkshire. Available loose, in bunches and in sachets.

www.shropshirelavender.co.uk – sells dried lavender grown in Shropshire. Available loose, in bunches and in sachets.

Acana Hanging Moth Killer and Wardrobe Freshener (with built-in indicator telling you when to replace them) – available from John Lewis, Lakeland, Hangerworld.

Moth pheromone traps – available from John Lewis, Lakeland, Amazon.

USEFUL ADDRESSES

www.rentokil.com

www.mothprevention.com

Specialist storage and garment care

Jeeves of Belgravia – vacuum packing and storage service for special garments Also sells acid-free tissue paper. See contact details under dry-cleaners. www.jeevesofbelgravia.co.uk

The Wardrobe Curator – seasonal storage of clothing. Other services include creating an online photographic wardrobe catalogue. Online shop sells a range of hangers, sweater bags, garment bags, acid-free tissue paper, folding templates, lingerie wash bags, anti-moth products and shoeboxes. www.thewardrobecurator.co.uk

Specialist dry-cleaners

Blossom and Browne Sycamore – dry-cleaner to the Queen. Many other services offered, including vintage and couture dry-cleaning service, repairs and alterations, leather and suede cleaning, handbag and shoe repairs. www.blossomandbrowne.com

Jeeves of Belgravia – specialist dry-cleaner and valeting service. Other services offered include repairs and alterations, leather and suede cleaning, shoe repair, luggage repair, climate-controlled garment storage, handbag restoration. Nine branches across London: Belgravia, Berkeley Square, Chelsea, Fleet Street, Hampstead, Kensington, Mayfair, Notting Hill, St Paul's. www.jeevesofbelgravia.co.uk

Connoisseur Dry-Cleaners – specialist dry-cleaner and supplier of acid-free storage boxes. Many other services offered, including repairs and alterations; leather and suede cleaning; ski wear cleaning; wax jacket cleaning; moth treatment. www.connoisseurdrycleaners.co.uk

Clothing alterations/mending

The Invisible Mending Service – family business in Marylebone, London, that has been running for 70 years. Repairs damaged clothing using re-weaving techniques (threads are extracted from a hidden section of the garment). www.invisible-mending.co.uk

Love Cashmere Care Service – repair service for knitwear made of cashmere and lambswool. www.cashmerecareservice.co.uk

Alterations Boutique – bespoke tailoring and garment alterations. www.alterationsboutique.co.uk

The Wardrobe Curator – re-styling and alterations of garments. Also offers seasonal storage of clothing. www.thewardrobecurator.co.uk

The Denim Doctor – repair and alteration service based in Manchester, specifically for denim garments. www.thedenimdoctor.co.uk

Clothing care advice

Textile Services Association – www.tsa-uk.org
Home Laundering Consultative Council – www.care-labelling.co.uk
Royal School of Needlework – repair and restoration of textiles. www.royal-needlework.co.uk
www.loveyourclothes.org.uk – advice on care, repair and recycling.

Useful laundry products

Stain removal

Amodex Ink and Stain Remover – available from the Pen Company. www.thepencompany.co.uk
Dascos – fabric cleaner for leather and suede. Available from www.dunkelman.com
De.Solv.It – natural citrus-based stain remover. www.desolvit.com
Stain Devils Stain Removers – target specific stains. www.dr-beckmann.co.uk
Sticky Stuff Remover – to remove glue, gum etc. Available from www.lakeland.co.uk
Tide to Go Stain Remover pen – portable stain remover pen. Available from www.amazon.com or other online retailers.
Shout Wipe and Go – portable stain removal wipes. Available from www.amazon.com or other online retailers.
Wine Away – removes red wine and other stains. Available from www.wineaway.com or www.lakeland.co.uk
Dylon White & Bright – prevents the greying of whites.

Mr Clean Magic Eraser – removes marks from trainers. Available from www.amazon.com and other online retailers.

Dylon Wash & Dye – to revive colour of faded jeans. Available from John Lewis.

Dylon Colour Catcher – allows for mixed-colour loads. Available from supermarkets.

Sewing suppliers

MacCulloch & Wallis – fabric and haberdashery supplier. www.macculloch-wallis.co.uk

John Lewis – haberdashery department. www.johnlewis.com

Care of accessories

Shoes

James Taylor & Son – bespoke shoemakers offering repair and restoration service, including resoling. www.taylormadeshoes.co.uk

Crockett & Jones – retail stores sell shoe-care products. www.crockettandjones.com

Russell & Bromley – retail stores sell shoe-care products. www.russellandbromley.co.uk

www.dunkelman.com – shoe-care products and advice. Instant shoe-shine sponges are available from most cobblers, shoe shops, www.amazon.com and most supermarkets.

Wellington boots

Hunter – sells Wellington boot care products. www.hunter-boot.com/care-products

Handbags

Handbag Clinic – restoration and repair service for leather handbags. They will also buy and re-sell unwanted designer handbags. Branches in London, Manchester, Newcastle and Leeds. Their services are also available through The Queen Bee boutique in Monaco. www.handbagclinic.co.uk

Hats

MILLINERY

Rachel Trevor-Morgan Millinery – royal warrant holder. Atelier is based in St James's, London. Hats and headpieces can be dyed to match your outfit. www.racheltrevormorgan.com

Rosie Olivia Millinery – elegant and stylish hats and headpieces, popular with the royal family. www.rosieoliviamillinery.com

Juliette Botterill Millinery – London-based milliner popular with the young British royals. www.juliettemillinery.co.uk

Jane Taylor London – London milliner popular with British and European royals. Bespoke and ready-to-wear. Stockists include Harrods, Fenwick and Fortnum & Mason. Flagship store is on the King's Road, Chelsea. www.janetaylorlondon.com

Lock Hatters – hat seller offering hat grooming and repair services. www.lockhatters.co.uk

Jewellery

Town Talk – sells a wide range of easy-to-use jewellery cleaning kits suitable for cleaning gold, silver and precious stones. www.towntalkpolish.com

Heming London – jewellery repairs, including pearl restringing. www.jewellery-repairs-london.co.uk

Personal shopping

Harrods – the 'By Appointment' service provides assistance with sourcing items. www.harrodsbyappointment.com

Fenwick – personal shopping service. www.fenwick.co.uk

Selfridges – offers a personal shopping service to assist with sourcing items. www.selfridges.com

Recycling/selling clothes

Cudoni – re-sells pre-owned luxury goods. They will collect and photograph the items for you; good-quality photos will always attract more custom, and a higher price. Cudoni emphasise their environmental focus, encouraging people to recycle unwanted quality garments that were made to last a lifetime; re-selling enables sustainability. www.cudoni.com

Rebelle – online marketplace for buying and selling second-hand designer clothing. The seller lists the item online and then sends to Rebelle, who will ship to the buyer once the garment is authenticated; 48-hour guaranteed delivery service. www.rebelle.com

Vestiaire Collective – French-born online marketplace to buy and sell luxury pre-owned fashion. All items are authenticated by in-house experts when sold, before sending to the buyer. www.vestiairecollective.com

Vinted – online market place for buying and selling new or second-hand clothing, high street and high end. The seller lists and dispatches the garment. www.vinted.co.uk

The Dresser – second-hand designer clothes shop. www.dresseronline.co.uk

HEWI London – online marketplace for second-hand designer clothing. www.hardlyeverwornit.com

Recycle Now – advice on how and where to recycle old clothes. www.recyclenow.com/reduce/love-your-clothes

Oxfam – With Marks & Spencer they have a 'Shwopping' initiative. www.oxfam.org.uk/donate/donate-goods/mands-and-oxfam-shwopping

Appendix II – Clothing care symbols

CARE SYMBOLS			
Symbol	Meaning	Symbol	Meaning
⊔	Washing process – machine or hand	○	Dry-cleaning
△	Chlorine bleaching	⊡	Tumble-drying
⌐	Ironing	✕	Do not

WASHING		
Symbol	Meaning	Notes
40° 60° 95°	Cotton wash	The number indicates the highest temperature it is safe to wash the garment.
40° 50°	Synthetics wash (single bar)	A single bar is shown under the wash tub to indicate reduced washing conditions at this temperature.
40°	Wool wash (double bar)	A double underline indicates minimum washing conditions at the temperature shown. Designed for machine-washable wool garments.
✋	Hand-wash only	Garment not suitable for washing machine conditions – must be hand-washed only.

DRY-CLEANING

Symbol	Meaning
Ⓟ Ⓕ Ⓦ	Must be professionally dry-cleaned. The letters contained within the circle, and/or a bar beneath the circle, will indicate the solvent and the process to be used by the dry-cleaner.
⊗	Do not dry-clean.

TUMBLE-DRYING

Symbol	Meaning
▢	May be tumble-dried.
▢••	Can be tumble-dried on a high heat setting.
▢•	Can be tumble-dried on a low heat setting.
⊠	Do not tumble-dry.

IRONING		BLEACHING	
Symbol	Meaning	Symbol	Meaning
🔥•••	Hot iron	△	Any bleach allowed
🔥••	Warm iron	⚠	Only oxygen bleach
🔥•	Cool iron	⊗	Do not bleach

Acknowledgements

I'm very grateful to Katie Bond and Amy Feldman of
the National Trust who originally took on my idea for
this book; Peter Taylor, Lucy Smith and the team at
Pavilion for their expert editing and transformation of
my manuscript; Graeme Clarke at Erddig for providing
fascinating details about Ladies' Maids in the service of
the Yorke family; Jennie Blythe and Gabriella Ossoinak
for their support and encouragement during the writing
process; Adélie for her flexibility looking after my dog,
Dorothy, when I was in-between France and England
(pugs are not the most cross-channel friendly of pooches);
and my twin sister Nicola for hugely contributing to the
book-in-progress, and reading through the manuscript
multiple times with her eagle eye. A special thanks to my
Dad for writing letters to me wherever I am in the world;
they are always gratefully received.

Picture Credits

INDEX

Alicia Healey has an MA in Art History from the University of St Andrews. She spent four years working for the Royal Household based at Buckingham Palace, before travelling the world as a Lady's Maid and Personal Assistant, visiting locations including Riyadh, Japan, Bali and the USA. She now works freelance as a Wardrobe Consultant and Stylist.